Beautiful
Ontario Towns

Fred Dahms

JAMES LORIMER & COMPANY LTD., PUBLISHERS
TORONTO, 2001

James Lorimer & Company Ltd. acknowledges the support of the Ontario Arts Council. We acknowledge the support of the Government of Canada through the Book Publishing Industry Development Program (BPIDP) for our publishing activities. We acknowledge the support of the Canada Council for the Arts for our publishing program.

Design and layout: Gwen North
Photo (top left) page 26: David Smiley

National Library of Canada Cataloguing in Publication Data

Dahms, Fred, 1935–
   Beautiful Ontario towns

Includes index.
ISBN 1-55028-713-3

1. Ontario, Southwestern – History. Local.* 2. Ontario, Southwestern – Description and travel,* I. Title.

FC3095.S68D33 2001   971.3'2 C00-933216-2
F1057.D33 2001

James Lorimer & Company Ltd., Publishers
35 Britain Street
Toronto, Ontario
M5A 1R7

Printed and bound in Canada.

ACKNOWLEDGEMENTS

During the writing of this book, my wife, Ruth, has been my literary critic, field assistant and companion. To her I extend my love, thanks and appreciation. Diane Young and Craig Saunders have contributed many helpful comments and suggestions.

CONTENTS

Southern Ontario

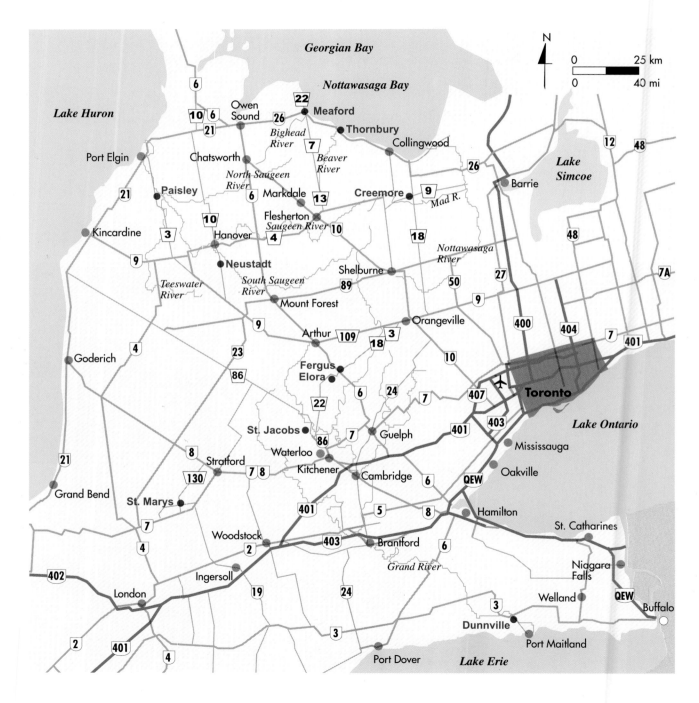

Georgian Bay

Nottawasaga Bay

Lake Huron

N

0   25 km
0   40 mi

Owen Sound
Meaford
Thornbury
Collingwood
Bighead River
Beaver River
Port Elgin
Chatsworth
North Saugeen River
Markdale
Creemore
Mad R.
Barrie
Lake Simcoe
Paisley
Flesherton
Saugeen River
Kincardine
Hanover
Neustadt
Teeswater River
South Saugeen River
Shelburne
Nottawasaga River
Mount Forest
Goderich
Arthur
Orangeville
Fergus Elora
Toronto
St. Jacobs
Guelph
Waterloo
Lake Ontario
Stratford
Kitchener
Cambridge
Mississauga
Oakville
Grand Bend
St. Marys
Hamilton
St. Catharines
Woodstock
Brantford
Niagara Falls
Ingersoll
Grand River
Welland
Buffalo
London
Dunnville
Port Maitland
Port Dover
Lake Erie

6

INTRODUCTION

In the 1960s, "small is beautiful" and "back to the land" were the slogans of hippies, drop-outs and draft-dodgers. Today these sentiments are echoed by professionals seeking a quiet residential haven and by retirees who wish to escape the noise and danger of busy cities. Off the throughways and along our country roads lie many of Ontario's most beautiful communities. They entice both tourists and permanent settlers. Diversity, complexity and change are the hallmarks of these repositories of local history, fascinating architecture and friendly people. Their early settlers took advantage of their rivers, falls, agricultural hinterlands and local building materials to create the settlements that we see today. In this book, you will discover some of the most attractive and interesting places in Ontario.

Selecting towns and villages to discuss was difficult, simply because there are so many in the province, and they are all so picturesque. Eventually, several criteria were used. Each had to be within a two-hour drive of the major cities of Southern Ontario. None were to have a population over ten thousand, and none were to be swamped by creeping urbanization. The architecture of each community had to reflect local geology and building materials. All had to be appealing to visitors and to those who might wish to move to them permanently. The selection needed to reflect the diversity and complexity of Ontario's beautiful rural communities. Local economies had to be healthy and attractive to potential migrants. All needed to be engaging, prosperous places with friendly residents and helpful merchants.

The fire tower and town hall, Paisley

Knox Presbyterian Church, Elora

The following places were finally chosen: Creemore, Dunnville, Elora, Fergus, Meaford, Neustadt, Paisley, St. Jacobs, St. Marys and Thornbury. In or near these communities, you will discover crafts, breweries, fine dining, historic limestone architecture, sandy beaches and outstanding fishing, skiing, hiking and caving. Like most Ontario settlements, all began at dam sights providing power for sawmills and gristmills. In many, these early industrial buildings have been recycled into trendy shops or restaurants. In some, local culture dominates, while elsewhere, entrepreneurial activity has transformed the character of the towns. Many offer historic properties and new homes at prices far lower than any in the city. All provide pleasure and stimulation for the day-tripper or

shopper, and affordable properties for those seeking a home away from the city.

Before we profile these ten communities, a little background will give us a deeper appreciation of their contemporary character. Each reflects the efforts of their earliest settlers, and to this day, their architecture and economies are inextricably linked to their original physical sites. To understand the present and future, we must know a little about the past. A brief portrait of Ontario's history and geology will provide this background.

THE PHYSICAL GEOGRAPHY OF ONTARIO

In the area roughly north of Barrie, the massive, glaciated granite surface of the Precambrian Shield dominates and provides the topography we all associate with "cottage country." Its rough, pockmarked surface is dotted with thousands of lakes carved by the glaciers and lined by the striations left when scraped by boulder-impregnated ice. Needless to say, little successful farming and few towns were established there, despite the efforts of the government and its colonization roads. Mining, forestry and tourism have traditionally dominated in this vast and sparsely settled region of Ontario.

South of the shield, the main physical feature is the edge of the Niagara Escarpment, which winds its way from Queenston to Tobermory and on to Manitoulin Island. In places such as Creemore or Flesherton, the escarpment is almost obliterated

Part of a large esker

by the deep glacial deposits that cover most of Southern Ontario. Elsewhere, as near Meaford, it towers over the countryside, dominating the local topography.

During the Wisconsin glacial period that ended some 15,000 years ago, much of Southern Ontario was either covered by water, ponded at the edge of vast masses of receding ice or was under the ice itself. The bedrocks of granite, limestone, sandstone and shale were abraded, ground, pulverized and sorted, finally to become the ingredients of the glacial deposits now covering most of Southern Ontario.

The surface landscape was carved, deposited and molded by towering, blue-white mountains of ice, sometimes a kilometre high. With changes in temperature and precipitation, they advanced and receded, either scraping bare slashes along protruding rocks as on the Bruce Peninsula, or dumping enormous piles of mixed sand, silt, clay and rock called till, which is found over most of the province south of the Precambrian Shield.

Where streams of water ran under the glacier, they filled with sand, boulders and silt, emerging finally as long sinuous ridges called eskers. Some remain today, but many have been destroyed by urban development, or mined for their sand and gravel. In pioneer days, they provided handy sources of building material for the settlers.

The glaciers that affected Ontario advanced in all directions from the Great Lakes basins, gouging and scraping the depressions to their present depth. Where water stood for long periods at the margins of the ice, silt, sand and clay were deposited to form gentle plains along the Erie shore as at Dunnville, from London to Windsor and around Lake Ontario.

The legacy of the Wisconsin glaciation has left relatively fertile land in much of Southern Ontario, which remains dotted with cigar-shaped hills called drumlins. They were formed when the moving ice rode over and streamlined the till beneath its base. Some excellent examples are found near St. Jacobs. Water, rock and till were left after glacial lobes receded, outlining their former position with a ring of tumbled, lake-studded moraines

The Niagara Escarpment near Creemore

By the 1600s, French missionaries and traders began to visit, followed by settlers from Britain and America. Ambitious men and women built their communities from the resources provided by nature and their predecessors. Construction materials employed by imaginative individuals and variations in local geology created settlements of remarkable diversity and complexity. In some towns limestone was the basic building material, while in others wood or fieldstone was employed. A few villages grew into major cities, but many retained their small-town character.

GROWTH AND DECLINE

By the end of the nineteenth century, many settlements had attained their largest populations, reflecting the prosperity of their rich rural hinterlands. On Saturday night the streets thronged with farmers who came to collect mail, shop and socialize at the tavern. Larger towns boasted handsome civic buildings attracting touring musicians and players. Victorian business blocks with towers and crenellations embellished their busy streets. Some grew into cities, but charm and heritage remain in those that were bypassed by the growth and "progress" of the twentieth century.

The beginning of rural mail delivery in 1916 and prohibition a few years later slowed development in many places. The taverns closed and farmers collected mail at the end of their lanes. Communities surviving these catastrophes were hit even harder by the increasing use of motor transport in the 1930s. Anyone with a vehicle could bypass the local service centre for a larger town with more choice and excitement. Many settlements stagnated or disappeared completely. Some with outstanding attractions or excellent entrepreneurs hung on to grow and thrive again.

RURAL RENAISSANCE

During the last twenty years, major revolutions have occurred in the countryside. The 100-acre farm has been supplanted by the 1,000-acre agribusiness. A few men and machines can now do the work that formerly employed large farm families. Many predicted that this would lead to the demise of our smaller places while metropolitan centres attracted all the growth. Indeed, some rural settlements did "die," but metropolitan development was not as rapid as predicted. New trends began to change the balance.

like those found near Neustadt and Creemore. The major moraines generally parallel the shores of lakes Huron and Ontario, although numerous examples exist across the province, especially inland from Meaford and Thornbury.

Elsewhere, sand plains, relatively level areas of glacial till and numerous lakes and swamps provide variety in topography, soil types and vegetation as well as potential for farming. St. Marys is situated on a glacial spillway where the limestone bedrock was exposed by water and became easy to extract. The evolution of each of the places discussed later in this book was affected profoundly by glacial events and by the underlying bedrock that preceded them. Their origins and economies were to a large extent the result of these pre-historic geological events.

THE COMING OF THE PEOPLE

During the Pleistocene Epoch, a mere million years ago, peoples of the First Nations wandered below the edges of the ice, hunting, fishing and gathering to stay alive. From this primeval environment they created the first communities.

Traditional rural service centres remain, especially off the major highways. Others have been transformed. Some villages have been gentrified with renovated heritage buildings and cobblestones or bricks on their streets. Others have experienced an influx of wealthy retirees to their gracious Victorian mansions. In scenic areas, cottages, chalets and condos are being built and renovated. Towns located beside lakes or rivers have been swamped by marinas. Summer residences are being converted to permanent homes. Crafts and antiques are featured in the general stores where once farm implements were sold.

TECHNOLOGY

Connecting a computer to a telephone line or fibre-optic cable has revolutionized our lives. We send messages or transmit exact images instantaneously across thousands of kilometres. No longer must we travel to the office. We can remain in contact from afar. Today the editor of a major newspaper may live in Thornbury, while a financial executive operates her business from a farm near Elora. E-mail connects us from anywhere on earth.

Even if we travel to a workplace, our job may no longer be in the city. More and more "footloose" industry has relocated in the countryside. Today, employees and executives live and work in villages or hamlets where they enjoy both rural amenities and access to a city. Satellite dishes enable remote communities to share information with sophisticated cities.

Cottagers, day-trippers and vacationers are a mobile population transferring wealth to villages and to the country. Recreation, shopping, scenery and employment are now available beyond the cities. With each visit or permanent move, some wealth is transferred from the old industrial heartland to the new "amenity frontier." Access to a city, scenery, heritage architecture or lower costs may transform a sleepy village into a centre of growth and development. Entrepreneurs make this happen.

LIFE ON THE NEW FRONTIER

Early retirement and flexible work days make it possible to live almost anywhere. We now demand more privacy, leisure time and amenities than ever before. Locational decisions are driven by aspirations for quality of life and a private piece of nature, especially among the affluent. Increasingly, there is a blurring of the boundaries between work and recreation. Families seek

environments that can enrich their lives while allowing them to maintain an adequate standard of living. Rejuvenated villages provide these conditions for many.

Even with attractive natural or heritage endowments, rejuvenation doesn't just happen. Some villages have languished for years and maps are dotted with settlements that stopped growing or just disappeared. But when someone with foresight, ambition and capital discovers an opportunity, economic miracles can occur. An individual who promotes summer theatre or a festival may start the ball rolling. Something as prosaic as excellent coffee and bran muffins at the general store will tempt travellers to tarry. The renovation of a building for artisans, or the conversion of a hotel into a country tavern can stimulate a local renaissance.

Many a sleepy settlement has been rejuvenated by a developer who builds homes less expensive than those in the city. Urban dwellers are lured by advertising that emphasizes the charm and rurality of a village. Entrepreneurs create retirement homes from former schools, mills, breweries, hotels or Victorian mansions. This stimulates the local pharmacy, adds life to the village historical society and provides volunteers for church groups. New citizens sometimes become innovative politicians with creative and original ideas. Local conflicts about community goals may occur, but the influx of enterprising people almost always provokes change and development.

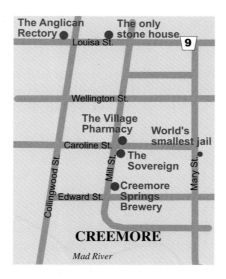

The Anglican Rectory • Louisa St. • The only stone house 9

Wellington St.

The Village Pharmacy • World's smallest jail

Caroline St. • The Sovereign

• Creemore Springs Brewery

Collingwood St. Mill St. Mary St.

Edward St.

CREEMORE

Mad River

CREEMORE: HILLS AND HISTORY

Creemore lies on the spillway of the Mad River in one of the most scenic areas of the province. This valley drops from an elevation of 518 metres at Badjeros to under 182 metres at its mouth. Any drive in the vicinity of Creemore takes you along winding valleys with rushing streams, through deep chasms and across rolling moraine. Dense forests are interspersed with farms where the land is level. The site of Creemore proper, being on the relatively level spillway, has little relief, but the village nestles comfortably below the escarpment and jumbled rolling moraine. Its environs are just as pretty, with places like Dunedin, Glen Huron and Singhampton close at hand.

EARLY HISTORY AND EUROPEAN SETTLEMENT

Even before the ice had receded completely, Palaeo-Indian hunters roamed the area around Creemore. As the ice receded at the end of the Pleistocene Epoch, the climate continued to

Left: *Mill Street*

warm, revealing more of the land that we know today. Natives in this Archaic Period were expert users of stone tools with which they hollowed logs for canoes and made adzes and axes. Their "banner stones," fashioned from slate, and cold-hammered copper spear points have been discovered near Creemore. By about 1,000 BC, lakes had reached contemporary levels and the Woodland Period began. By the end of this period, innovative fishing, hunting and corn horticulture had arrived in Nottawasaga Township.

After 1616, the French, who were still searching for China and promoting the fur trade, travelled to the area. They encountered the Iroquois and Ottawa Algonquins, who had left their beaver-depleted homelands to colonize this fur-rich area south of Georgian Bay. Samuel de Champlain and Father Joseph le Caron noted nine Indian villages between Creemore and Craigleith, inexplicably naming the Indians of the principal village Nation de Petun (tobacco people). It is believed that this village where Champlain stayed was on the south-facing hill

13

behind the old Anglican manse, overlooking Creemore and the Mad River valley.

Unfortunately, war and imported diseases ravaged the Petuns, and by the time the Jesuits arrived in 1639, the former large villages were gone. By 1650, the Indian survivors deserted the area entirely, to be replaced only sporadically by Ojibwa, who conducted seasonal hunting and fishing expeditions there. They surrendered the territory to the British Crown in 1818.

THE FOUNDING

Creemore was founded after a successful industrialist from Gananoque, John McDonald, was granted approximately twenty-seven lots in Nottawasaga Township between 1837 and 1844. In those days, settlers were required to clear half the road allowance in front of their property and to arrange for mills to be built. McDonald recruited William Nutly from Gananoque to guide settlers to lots for resale and to begin construction of mills. Nutly convinced his brother-in-law, Edward Webster, and Webster's younger brother George to come and help with the construction.

Edward Webster bought a boat to carry his family, a sawmill outfit, a run of stones, a flutter water-wheel and a carding mill. They travelled from Gananoque to Creemore via Lake Ontario, the newly built Welland Canal, lakes Erie and St. Clair and Lake Huron. Then they sailed around the Bruce Peninsula and up the Nottawasaga River as far as it was navigable. The last few tortuous miles were by ox cart through rough country and dense underbrush, which had to be cut to reach Creemore. By 1845 Nutly and the Websters had built a mill on the Mad River. The Land Agent's house was soon joined by a Presbyterian church and the Purple Hill Orange Lodge, on the top of the moraine now known as Hunter's Ridge.

INDUSTRY AND COMMERCE

Below the hill was the millpond, sawmill and a blacksmith's shop. Soon these were joined by a store, a post office in 1849, a grist-mill and a flour mill. By the 1850s, a busy industrial area, including a carding and fulling mill, a bedstead and chair factory, a blacksmith, and a potash works, had been established near the millpond. With this rapid growth, Webster anticipated a thriving

An estate below Hunter's Ridge

village and quickly had his land surveyed into town lots, which he sold to new arrivals. When the post office opened, another Irish countryman, Judge James Gowan, gave the settlement the name Creemore (which also means "big heart" in Gaelic) after a town in Wexford.

According to the 1871 census, Creemore had a postmaster, a doctor, two servants, two ministers, two lumbermen, two merchants, two hotelkeepers, a weaver, two saddlers, two shoe-makers, one milliner, one blacksmith, one cooper, one clerk, a few farmers and some women and children. The total population had reached 300. The hotels were popular places and pioneers told of Kelly's tavern lined from wall to wall with "recumbent drunks." The Traveler's Inn advertised itself as a "House that is pleasantly situated and affords every accommodation. The best brands of Wines, Liquors, and Cigars. Good Stabling. The vicinity is unequalled for trout fishing." The Simcoe County Directory in 1872 called Creemore a "village pleasantly situated in the midst of beautiful and prolific country ... the Mad River flows through the village and affords first class power. The vicinity is remarkably healthy and is a favourite resort for health and pleasure-seekers." These words were a forecast of things to come.

CHANGE AND DEVELOPMENT

Spirited debate accompanied the discussion in 1883 of whether or not to separate from the township and incorporate as a Police Village. The principal argument was about whether to include the river and the land to the south. Opponents claimed that the three bridges were always in danger of being destroyed by spring floods, and that their inclusion would add great expense to the village since they "did not last longer than five years before being swept away." The replacement cost, now borne by the township, would then become a responsibility of the village and might cost $1,000 over a ten-year period, thus raising local taxes. The discussion raged on until 1889 when the county council in Barrie debated the issue of incorporation and the cost of bridge main-tenance. A bylaw was finally passed on November 20 that year, stating that the "Village of Creemore containing seven hundred and fifty-three inhabitants" be incorporated into a separate corporation. Joseph Hood, who was one of the two delegates appointed by the citizens of Creemore to petition the county for incorporation, was appointed returning officer, for the village's first municipal election.

THE HISEY FAMILY AND THE "HOG SPECIAL"

In 1880 the Hisey family started a butcher shop now known as the Creemore Meat Market. They initially sold dressed hog carcasses to local residents, but soon saw the potential profit in exports. When the Freeman Packing House opened in Hamilton, the Hiseys began buying and selling hogs and ship-ping their carcasses to Hamilton on the Hamilton and North Western Railway line. Then a packing plant opened in Collingwood and local farmers rushed into the lucrative hog-raising business, selling their animals to the Hiseys for export. The average weekly shipment at the height of hog production was thirty railway cars (many double-decked) to Collingwood. There were so many pig-filled cars passing over the tracks that the train was commonly known as the "Hog Special."

In the early 1880s, John Hisey noticed a vein of red clay near his home. He built four kilns and a press to begin producing brick. Pressed bricks were to be used for interior walls while those fired in the kiln could withstand the weather and were for outside walls. Most of the earlier homes in the village were constructed of Hisey brick, but in a few cases, unscrupulous builders mixed pressed and fired brick to save on construction costs. The softer pressed brick is conspicuous because it has weathered more than its more durable fired counterpart and is therefore thinner, leaving brick-sized indentations wherever it was used. Brick-making ended when the clay supply ran out in 1912.

The 1880 home of the Hisey family butcher shop, now the Creemore Meat Market

A canopy of sugar maples

In 1900, John's brothers, Sam and Jake Hisey built a large grain elevator on the railway and a modern office on the main street. Since there was no bank in town, the vault at their office was used to store large amounts of cash to pay the farmers and functioned as a bank for short periods when people had cash to deposit. In 1905, the Hiseys added a potato house and apple cold-storage facility that could handle 20,000 barrels. They were instrumental in acquiring one of the first piped water systems in Ontario for the community in 1905. Eventually Sam Hisey moved to Toronto and became the "Potato King" of Ontario. The Hiseys' business continued under various ownership until 1970, when the grain elevator burned to the ground, ending a long saga in the history of Creemore.

THE WARS

The First World War called many young men from the village, some to be trained at nearby Camp Borden. During those years, milk was delivered in a handcart for six cents a quart and a taxi service ran between Creemore and Camp Borden. Local women made hospital gowns from old sheets, sewed and knit socks. Some also provided entertainment for the soldiers at Borden. Great rejoicing accompanied the end of the war, but in 1919 a virulent epidemic of influenza swept the county, taking more lives in Creemore than did all the battles of the war.

Post-war prosperity brought Model T Fords, Chevrolets and Buicks, fresh from their assembly lines, to the village. Ten gaso-line pumps, four garages and three car dealers lined the main street. Between 1912 and 1926, hydro was gradually introduced to the village. When the Ontario Hydro Company took over in 1916, the woollen mill on Caroline Street that had supplied power became redundant.

Saturday was shopping night. Farmers and citizens found all their requirements right in the village. Nine grocery stores, two hardware stores and two ice cream parlours joined the mills, barber shops and building supply factory in the village. A balance of retail, service and manufacturing activities kept the economy healthy.

The Noisy River Telephone Company, once the largest incorporated business in Creemore, was established by a group of farmers looking for better service. At first it was attached to Bell facilities in Creemore, but in 1926 it purchased Bell's lines and plant and began twenty-four hour service with the lowest rates in Ontario. The company grew and thrived until 1956, when faced with major expenses to implement a dial system, it was sold back to Bell.

During the Great Depression, Creemore suffered, but not as badly as larger places more dependent on financial services and factory employment. The Second World War brought renewed prosperity through a building boom at Camp Borden and a local trucking company that transported goods to the camp. Despite some hardships, the community thrived during the war.

CONTEMPORARY CHARACTER

Creemore's tree-lined streets and gracious houses reflect its proud mercantile heritage, while the business section of Mill Street personifies its developing functions. A canopy of glorious sugar maples shades the northern entrance of Mill Street and spreads to adjoining residential areas. A bookstore in a red-brick Victorian house with corbled-brick corners stands across the street from a potter and iron worker.

Farther south, the Creemore Springs Brewery in the former May Hardware building makes some of the best lager in Ontario. Its trucks stop regularly to obtain fresh water from a spring just outside town. This is a craft brewery that produces its beer in small batches brewed in open-fired kettles with no additives or preservatives. The brewery has become an important local attraction as well as a thriving business that sells beer across much of the province.

The Village Pharmacy is the oldest established business remaining in Creemore. The building was constructed in 1879 for John Carruthers and became W. J. Corbett's drug store in 1880.

Farther along Mill Street, the Creemore Meat Market remains much as it was in the 1800s. Local red kiln-fired brick was used to construct this delightful edifice, spoiled somewhat by a modern storefront. Nevertheless, the intricate pattern of yellow brick continues to adorn the second storey. The town's clock and watch store attracts customers from across the province. It occupies the building that was originally Plugsley's Harness Shop and now has a double storefront salvaged from the former Singhampton Post Office when it was demolished. This business, which builds, repairs and restores all manner of clocks from tiny mantel pieces to giant grandfathers, attracts customers from across Ontario.

House with decorative corbling

Not all Creemore's hotels have disappeared. The Sovereign was one of three that thrived with the arrival of the railway in 1877. It accommodated salesmen with their displays of merchandise and farmers coming to deliver their grain or hogs. The three arched doors at the back were the stables for the many teamsters who jammed the dining room and pub after making deliveries to the village. The different roof lines reflect three periods of expansion, but like so many of its contemporaries, the hotel closed with the coming of the car. Subsequently it was divided into apartments and used for a medical practice. Today it houses a restaurant specializing in Hungarian cuisine.

In addition to splendid homes and business blocks, Creemore boasts the "world's smallest jail." Unlike the majority of local buildings, it is constructed of limestone and split-field-stone facing.

The Mad River Pottery Company occupies a former creamery at 113 Mill Street. Hisey's home at 224 Mill Street is one of the most impressive, with its red brick, pillars, bay windows and intricate bracketing. The white building just behind it is the former carriage house. The second manse for the United Church occupies two lots at 194 Mill Street.

The Anglicans built their rectory in the "suburbs" at 32 Louisa Street. The present Anglican Church was built on Caroline Street in 1886. Farther along at 16 Louisa is the only stone house in the village. Built with 0.6-metre-thick walls in 1891, its simple Georgian design retains all original parts and windows. Fieldstone gathered from the site was used in its construction.

Creemore residents have cleverly capitalized upon their legacy of historic buildings and a tree-shaded site without spoiling the village. Despite some peripheral development, it remains a quiet country village in the midst of some of the most spectacular scenery in Ontario. It is easily accessible to the beaches of Georgian Bay, the challenging cross-country ski trails at Kolapore and downhill skiing at Mansfield or Collingwood. The Bruce Trail and a series of quaint villages on rushing streams are also nearby. Creemore is an ideal retreat for a day, a week or retirement.

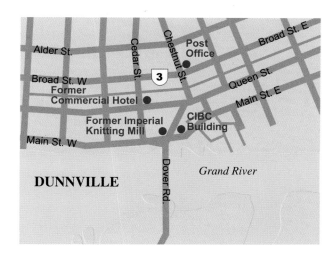

DUNNVILLE: RIVER TOWN

Dunnville's location on the north shore of Lake Erie provided access to the interior via the Grand River, and after 1825, connections to the world through the Great Lakes and Welland Canal. Today, Highway 3 bisects the town and runs east to Fort Erie sixty kilometres away. The town is surrounded by glacial deltas and shorelines, on which developed excellent soils for agriculture, a mainstay of the economy even today. The limestone beneath is relatively easy to excavate, and in the early years supplied considerable building stone and lime to local construction. It also contained natural gas, which was discovered in Dunnville in 1891 and has remained an important resource to this day.

By 1915, the Haldimand Gas Field was the second-most important in Ontario. Although most of the old wells have been depleted and shut down, modern techniques and the extension of drilling under Lake Erie have resulted in continued production of natural gas in the area. Much of Dunnville's early economic success can be attributed to the exploitation of its limestone and natural gas resources.

EARLY HISTORY

The natives of the area were the Petuns, Hurons and Neutral

Left: *Rigg Mansion*

Indians, who also lived around Georgian Bay. Artifacts indicate that they inhabited the region for thousands of years until they were wiped out by the Iroquois in 1650. For the next hundred years there were visits by Mississauga tribes, who camped along the river, but no permanent settlements. However, excavations have unearthed artifacts from the earlier periods dating to before the time of Christ.

Many historians believe that the first white man to paddle along the Grand was Étienne Brûlé in 1616. By then there were again many natives in the area; some estimated that there were as many as 12,000 Neutrals living in over forty villages. The first white men to pass Dunnville and enter the lake were two French priests, Father Jean de Brébeuf and Father d'Allion. Having set out from Georgian Bay on October 18, 1626, they reached the Grand River on December the 8th and remained in the area of Dunnville for three months. Subsequently, other priests travelled there and remarked upon the abundance of wildlife:

> There is an incredible number of stags, a great abundance of moose and elk, beaver, wildcats and black squirrels, a great quantity of wild geese, turkeys, cranes and other animals which are there all winter. The rivers furnish excellent fish, the earth gives good

A natural gas well

THE IMPACT OF THE WELLAND FEEDER CANAL

Building the canals provided employment for local workers and the feeder canal's abundant water power stimulated industry. Shops, blacksmiths, hotels and churches were soon established to accommodate the new arrivals. A carding mill, brewery, taverns and several distilleries began to do a roaring business. The settlement now had an excellent power source and was becoming a business and manufacturing centre.

The damming of the river made it navigable as far upstream as Cayuga. Boats could travel from Lake Ontario, through the Welland Canal to the Feeder to Dunnville and Cayuga. Paddle wheelers took passengers from Dunnville to Brantford for a dollar, supposedly in twenty-two hours. Unfortunately, high winds often blew the boats into shallow water along the Grand, causing lengthy delays. A series of swing bridges was built to accommodate river traffic, but the Grand River Navigation Company abandoned service because of financial difficulties in the early 1870s.

Shipping on the river through Dunnville to Port Maitland accommodated most of the surplus lumber and farm produce from a large area north of Lake Erie. Businesses were established in Dunnville to process, pack and service this important trade, leading to increased business for other merchants and manufacturers in the area. Steady growth ensued and at the turn of the century, Dunnville reached a population of 2,700. By 1903 four textile manufacturers had set up, taking advantage of the inexpensive electricity and natural gas in the area. Even during the Depression of the 1930s, Dunnville fared better than many other Ontario communities.

grain and they (the natives) have squashes, beans and other vegetables in abundance.

According to early travellers, the low-lying land and swamps were also inhabited by "large and ferocious mosquitoes."

THE BEGINNINGS OF DUNNVILLE

Dunnville was originally part of the Township of Moulton and began about a kilometre south of its present location. By 1825, there were only six houses in Dunnville when William Hamilton Merritt chose it as the western terminus of the Welland Feeder Canal. Dunnville was named after John Henry Dunn, Receiver General for Upper Canada, who was also a friend and supporter of Merritt's canal scheme. A dam, called T'KaneKhodth by the natives (meaning big dam) was built to facilitate the flow of water from Lake Erie to fill the new Welland Canal, which bypassed Niagara Falls. Its construction and that of the feeder stimulated growth in the fledgling community. Initially much of the population consisted of labourers working on the waterways. They came and went but contributed considerably to the local economy. From 1829 to 1846, the population of Dunnville oscillated around 400.

BRIDGES

Bridges were very important to Dunnville's development, as the Grand River complicated early land transportation. Originally there was a ferry crossing at Dunnville but it was slow and expensive. The first toll bridge, which followed the dam, was built in 1834. Cost overruns caused tolls to be higher than anticipated, but, at fifteen cents for a team of horses, ten cents for one horse and two cents for pedestrians, it was a small price to pay. The bridge eliminated a sixty-nine-kilometre diversion through Hamilton and Brantford for travellers from Fort Erie.

The last toll house was erected in 1852. Thereafter, Dunnville's bridges were often washed away or damaged by spring floods, leading to long periods during which they were repaired or replaced. Travellers once again had to revert to the slow and expensive ferry. The original bridge was replaced four times before a more substantial structure was built in 1918. A new bridge at the foot of Queen Street replaced it in 1964.

ROAD TRAVEL

The Canadian National Railway abandoned the last line through Dunnville in 1985, ending 130 years of railway service to the community. Roads had been important since the 1830s, but were very poor. They were quagmires in wet seasons and often bumpy and rutted. By the late 1800s, destinations not served by the railway were connected by roads, but even in 1885, travel by sled in the winter was much easier than that in other seasons. Streets in Dunnville remained in a deplorable condition, despite heavy use. By 1884, sidewalks were in reasonably good repair.

Cedar and Broad streets

The first paved road in Dunnville was constructed in 1912. When automobiles began to appear in 1898, they travelled at their own risk. Dunnville profited from the manufacture and repair of coaches, wagons and later automobiles. In 1913 a shipping company that grew out of a horse-drawn freight operation opened and eventually became one of the largest trucking firms in the province. Because the shortest route between Buffalo and Detroit is through Canada, heavy truck traffic continues to pass through Dunnville. During the Second World War, convoys continually travelled Highway 3 through the community.

RECENT DEVELOPMENT

Dunnville's population increased to 4,750 in 1950, and was recorded as 11,262 in 1974, when its boundaries were expanded to include rural areas (30,288 hectares) with the creation of the Regional Municipality of Haldimand-Norfolk. Within the historic urban area of Dunnville there are 5,033 persons, a slight drop from the 5,458 of 1974. Today, published census statistics are totally misleading, reflecting suburban and rural growth in the region outside the original municipality, which has retained its historic character.

Dunnville's contemporary character is the product of earlier growth and prosperity. Magnificent houses and businesses from the turn of the century survive and add to its charm. The river and nearby lake have lost some of their commercial importance but are now major tourist attractions.

ADVERSITY AND REJUVENATION

Dunnville faced some tough times in the 1960s and 70s as the Victoria Hotel burnt, and Monarch Knitting Mills went into receivership in 1967. During the following year, the mills were demolished except for a building near the water. This yellow brick structure, built in 1900, was originally the site of the Imperial Mill (called the White Mill).

By the 1980s, business terminations, high taxes and pollution were posing additional problems for the community. Fortunately, this was also a period of increased interest in history and the environment. Visitors came to explore downstream from the dam, camp in the conservation areas, swim, fish, boat and enjoy the casual ambience of a well-preserved country town. Readers Cafe on Queen Street, with its fifties juke box, collection of antique books and excellent snacks, personifies the small-town atmosphere and friendly service available in Dunnville.

A Harvard Mark II airplane memorializes the 47 pilots killed while training at the RCAF Flying School.

St. Michael's Roman Catholic Church

SOME HISTORIC SITES

Dunnville's historic business streets converge at Queen, Main and Chestnut, which is the commercial heart of the community. The elegant Bank of Hamilton on Queen Street was built initially as the Scott Block in 1901. In 1922 it was renovated into the dignified Italian Renaissance structure now occupied by the CIBC. The former Rexall building, the millennium sculpture and nearby 1936 post office make this a very attractive area. Just along Chestnut Street in front of the library, a Harvard Mark II aircraft commemorates the forty-seven pilots killed in training accidents as they trained at the RCAF Flying School in Dunn Township (now part of Dunnville).

A few blocks away, houses of great architectural distinction, some built by leading early merchants, as well as schools and churches on the quiet tree-lined streets, reflect the community's prosperous past. A Chamber of Commerce walking tour guides visitors through old Dunnville. Mansions from the glory days at the turn of the century line Cedar, Broad and Alder streets. The former Commercial Hotel at 116 Lock Street is now a residence. The late Georgian-style Rigg mansion at 119 Broad Street features stained-glass windows and ornate porches. It stood at the very edge of the commercial district on the former Forks Road.

The Lalor residence built on Broad Street in 1905/6 was the social hub of Dunnville. Its splendid parties were attended by everyone from local dignitaries to prime ministers. Francis Ramsey Lalor began in the dry goods business and soon diversified to own the largest apple evaporator in North America. He exported dried apples and white vinegar and eventually obtained the controlling interest in Monarch Mills. He also served as reeve and local MP. At the corner of Cedar and Broad streets, the Smith family built their 1914 home on a high foundation to avoid the frequent floods. Until the 1950s, water often reached Broad Street in the spring. The Smiths, who owned the Reliable Drugstore, were also prominent citizens of Dunnville.

CONTEMPORARY CHARACTER

Today, marinas and condominiums along the river tempt visitors. Local developers are working hard to promote Dunnville as a major retirement and tourist community. Boat excursions, rentals and fishing expeditions are offered on the lake and river.

Visitors marvel at the power of the river frothing over the dam. A large anchor rescued from Lake Erie commemorates the intrepid sailors who struggled through dangerous storms on the lake to bring cargo to the town. Just ten minutes down the river, Port Maitland recalls the importance of fishing and river traffic in the nineteenth century. Its dock and lighthouse have seen better days, but remain as a constant reminder of Dunnville's nautical past.

Dunnville's membership in a sophisticated regional municipality has resulted in excellent social services and planning. Its favourable location and mild climate contribute substantially to its appeal. The mainstays of its robust economy are now manufacturing, agriculture, retail trade, construction, health and social services. Despite being politically part of a larger community, Dunnville retains the atmosphere of a rural service centre. Modern shopping, new bungalows and excellent medical facilities make it particularly attractive to visitors, commuters and those seeking a quiet place to retire.

Lalor House

Port Maitland

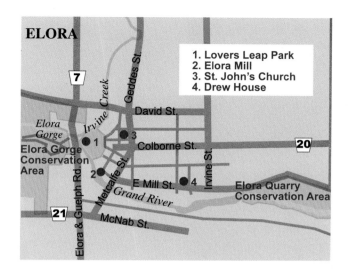

ELORA: MILL TOWN

Elora is about an hour's drive north-west of Toronto on a deep limestone gorge carved by the Grand River. Only four kilometres from its fascinating Scottish rival, Fergus, it is one of the most attractive communities in Ontario. Physically it is enhanced by the historic gorge and culturally it boasts the Elora Festival and many heritage homes.

The gorge was formed when the Grand and its glacial predecessors slowly dissolved a deep chasm into the soluble Guelph Formation of the Lockport Dolomite, cutting through the cap rock and tilted strata below. The gorge and its falls have been crucial to the past development and contemporary prosperity of the town.

EARLY HISTORY

For years the Elora Gorge and its caves had been sacred to the native peoples of Ontario. As the Iroquois swept across Southern Ontario, local Indian bands took shelter in this rugged six-kilometre limestone chasm at the confluence of the Grand River and Irvine Creek. Following the historic battle between the Hurons and Iroquois near what is now Hamilton in 1651, the local Neutral Indians hid their precious wampum

Left: *The Elora Mill Inn*

beads in a cave downstream from the site of Elora. After a heavy rain in 1880, two local boys discovered several of the beads that had washed out of the cave. They now rest in the Royal Ontario Museum in Toronto.

Elora's site had been visited as early as 1817 by travellers who remarked on the scenic beauty of the cataract where the river tumbled over a limestone ledge into the narrow gorge below. They also recognized its potential for power. In that year, Roswell Mathews, a Welshman from the United States, attempted to construct a dam, which washed away in the spring. Unable to grind wheat locally, he and his sons hollowed out a log and floated it with sixteen sacks of wheat downstream to Galt. There they sold the wheat for fifty cents a bushel and the dugout for $2.50. This incident ended attempts to settle Elora until the arrival of Captain William Gilkinson.

CAPTAIN WILLIAM GILKINSON

In 1832, Captain William Gilkinson of Irvine, Scotland, purchased a 14,000-acre tract for seven shillings and sixpence per acre and established Elora. Gilkinson was a cousin of John Galt, founder of Guelph and Goderich. With his considerable ambition and ample funds, Gilkinson provided Elora with excellent leadership and investment until his untimely death a

The Elora Gorge

year later. Elora languished, but grew again after 1844 when Charles Allan arrived, formed a company, purchased land and built a gristmill and several stores. Before his arrival it was not uncommon for settlers to walk to Dundas, Hamilton or Galt for a sack of flour or provisions. From the time of the building of the mill until the turn of the century, Elora competed successfully for business in the trade area that it shared with Fergus. Its settlers had finally used its water power effectively.

ECONOMIC RIVALRY

In 1846, Elora had only sixteen enterprises, primarily retail stores and mills. By 1881, its population stood at 1,387 with thirty-three businesses. When it became the northern terminus of the Credit Valley Railway it reached an all-time high of seventy-two businesses in 1891. Between 1891 and 1911 Elora lost twenty-three businesses primarily because of motor transport and competition from Fergus.

Elora is only four kilometres downstream from Fergus, but its economic development took a different turn from that of its nearby rival. Despite the fact that Elora and Fergus were established within two years of each other (1832 and 1834), their economic histories diverged considerably. Fergus has never exploited its geological assets as effectively as Elora. Fergus developed a formidable economic base, and is experiencing rapid population growth, but it has tended to underestimate the charm of its richly ornamented limestone buildings, falls and mills. In contrast, Elora's promotional literature emphasizes its heritage architecture and its physical setting. The town has developed a successful festival, house tours, river rafting and boutique shopping, whereas Fergus lags somewhat in comparable tourist attractions.

RIVER RENAISSANCE

For those who have visited Elora recently, its rebirth is not a mystery. Blessed by a magnificent site on a waterfall and a rocky gorge, it has always been something of a tourist attraction. For years visitors have stood at the Lover's Leap lookout above the confluence of the Grand River and Irvine Creek to marvel at the water and caves below.

The climb down the stairs between algae-covered boulders to the river has been a popular local pastime for years. In the cool of the gorge, water drips from the overhang and trickles slowly to the river. During the winter, long, sleek fingers of ice reach to the valley floor, clutching at the snow. Water swirls under the ice, making delicate patterns, eddies and whorls as it struggles to soar through the few open patches. Stalactites and stalagmites of crystallized precipitation cover the gray limestone chasm, imparting mystery and icy charm to this world of white and green.

An older home

The pond behind Mill Street

Mill Street

PIONEERING ENTREPRENEURS

The cataract and gorge continue to be important attractions for locals and tourists alike, but it took entrepreneurial effort and vision to transform a sleepy mill town into a major tourist attraction. After falling far behind its rival, Fergus, the real renaissance came only when several entrepreneurs realized the potential of Mill Street and began to restore its derelict industrial buildings. The lure of natural phenomena alone was inadequate to attract crowds of well-heeled visitors. So entrepreneurs took over, to enhance (or exploit, if you listen to the critics), the already attractive local environment.

The restoration and conversion of the Elora mill to an inn were a turning point for the village. Until 1972, it had functioned as a fully operating water-powered mill; one of the largest in the province. After several changes of ownership, this crumbling five-storey structure, strategically poised above the plunging falls, was lovingly rebuilt from top to bottom.

Inside the bar, along an exposed rocky outcrop, the original penstock (a pipe carrying water from the millrace) remains, now supplying the small hydro electric generator below. The exterior walls are one-and-a-half metres thick, while original beams grace the cosy dining room and antique-furnished bedrooms. In the winter, enormous fireplaces in the public rooms provide warmth and charm. From the windows and balcony, the Tooth of Time in the centre of the churning cataract dominates the scene.

The restoration was not accomplished easily. Financial hard-ship and opposition plagued what ultimately became the corner-stone of the "Mill Street Revival." Both the Ontario Heritage Foundation and the publication *Canada Country Inns* have acknowledged the excellence of the mill's restoration. It remains the economic anchor of Mill Street and an attraction in itself.

THE MILL STREET REVIVAL

In 1978, a Guelph company purchased land that formerly housed factories on the north side of the street just east of the mill. The remains of limestone walls were incorporated into a courtyard that now houses a variety of clothing, craft and candy shops.

In 1982, extensive renovations were made to what was once the stable, located directly by the cliff just downstream from the mill. This structure had been built in the traditional style of the time, with thick stone walls built to withstand the elements over the centuries. A cafe and outdoor seating area made from the wheels that used to drive the mill machinery were constructed from the ruins of the stable. A viewing platform overlooking the limestone Tooth of Time provides photo opportunities that had not existed for over a hundred years because the site had been inaccessible after the building of the mill.

Slowly at first, and then with increasing momentum, the initial risks paid off. Tourists arrived to buy antiques, view the scenery and dine on the balconies and patios by the river. Soon artists and artisans joined the local shopkeepers, making and selling their wares in and around the original Mill Street nucleus. Then buses from Toronto and Kitchener began to crowd the village with shoppers and tourists from June to October. By the mid-1980s, all the Mill Street establishments catered to tourists, while residents generally shopped farther north on Metcalfe and Geddes streets.

From its Mill Street genesis, the original tourist nucleus has crept up the hill along Metcalfe Street, almost reaching Geddes. Several new developments including the Village Commons have appeared. The Commons took advantage of a board and batten residence to accommodate eight shops offering antiques, handcrafted wooden pieces, jewellery and clothing. On the northern edge of town an antique warehouse was constructed on the site of a former lumberyard and farmers' market. It was opened in 1994, and is now home to sixty-four vendors in 4,500 square metres of space.

THE FESTIVAL

Elora has also fostered the performing arts. The Three Centuries Festival was established in 1979 to promote local artists and take

St. John's Anglican Church

advantage of acoustically excellent church sanctuaries. It presented instrumental and choral music primarily from the Renaissance period. The choir of St. John's Anglican Church led by Noel Edison became its mainstay. Recently the Festival choir has become a professional group called the Festival Singers, who join with Canadian and international artists to present a wide variety of music. Now called the Elora Festival, its performances are housed in the town's churches and restaurants. A "fringe festival" of talented local artists provides music and other entertainment along Elora's streets between major shows. Tea with the vicar under the tent beside St. John's Anglican Church has become a regular part of the festival experience.

A particularly attractive Festival event has been the quarry concert. On a warm summer evening crowds take to bleachers lining the cliffs above a man-made lake. Recently, the Festival has added popular singers such as Sarah McLachlan to its quarry series with great success. Unfortunately, inclement weather occasionally wreaks havoc upon the "quarry experience."

Another unique Festival experience is found in the township works depot, an "acoustically perfect concert hall." The birds that swirl and flit across the ceiling, seemingly keeping time and tune with the orchestra and chorus, contribute to the country setting. Despite uncomfortable folding metal chairs, which are used to seat patrons in what is essentially a barn, the opening and closing Festival gala performances staged there are inevitably sold out. The Elora Festival has become one of Canada's premier musical events, drawing crowds from across North America to a wide variety of classical, pop, folk and dramatic performances. For three weeks from mid-July, Elora is filled with music-lovers, and its shops are busier than usual.

CONTEMPORARY CHARACTER

Impressive residential architecture is found along Elora's side streets. Guided interior tours present a wealth of historic Ontario. In much of Elora, careful attention has been paid to the restoration of significant architecture. The Drew House was the residence of George Drew, premier of Ontario. Now it is an elegant bed and breakfast. Rosemount Cottage was the original home of St. John's School, an exclusive private academy. The liquor store occupies a carefully renovated drill hall built in 1865.

Although Elora's Gothic Revival churches are not as grand as those in Fergus, they remain important to the community.

St. John's (1875) provides an intimate setting for soloists and chamber groups while St. Mary's (1870) accommodates choral events during the Festival. It is reported that the Reverend John Smithhurst, an early pastor of St. John's, was the lover and first cousin of Florence Nightingale. Precluded from marriage by being related, Florence Nightingale went to Crimea to tend to the wounded while the reverend became a pastor in Elora. The silver communion set in the church is reputed to be a gift from Florence Nightingale. Knox Presbyterian Church (1873) stands in its own square, the steeple clearly visible from afar. Chalmers Presbyterian Church (1876) has become a private residence.

Rosemount Cottage

The community now boasts many skilled artists and artisans, including potters, glass blowers, painters and sculptors. Shops on Mill Street offer custom gold and silver, knitting, woollen products, brass rubbing and antiques. The authenticity of local products contrasts with the offerings in many larger tourist communities. Despite, or possibly because Elora could not compete for industry with Fergus, it has attracted a large and thriving community of artists and artisans.

In the winter, the scenery and trails at the Conservation Authority Park attract skiers and hikers. In summer it provides campsites and swimming. In addition to being the site of

Abandoned mill

Festival concerts, the quarry is a spectacular swimming hole on the road to Fergus. The Wellington County Museum on the same road is an ornate relic from the past, the former Wellington County House of Refuge. Now restored, it accommodates offices and an excellent local history collection.

THE FUTURE

Despite its obvious charm, Elora has not yet reached the status of Niagara-on-the-Lake as a tourist attraction. On the other hand, it appeals to increasing numbers and could easily become too "touristy." On some summer afternoons, buses and cars jam Mill Street, making access almost impossible.

Increasing numbers of businesses, tourists and residents have the potential to change Elora from a delightful country town into a "tourist trap." The balance between becoming a Niagara-on-the-Lake, where development has radically altered the social and economic fabric of the community, and retaining Elora's original charm is delicate. A number of local elections have been fought on the "growth versus no-growth" issue, the latest threat being the establishment of a race track complete with gambling facilities.

Only through consultation, cooperation and foresight will its citizens preserve the best of Elora while avoiding the worst excesses seen elsewhere. Today, it is one of Ontario's finest examples of a well-preserved mill and tourist town from the 1870s. Its attractions are well worth a visit of several days.

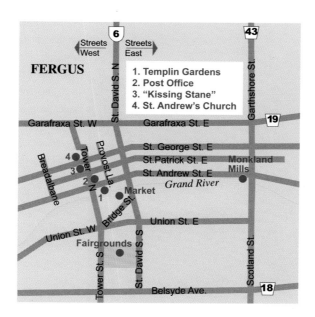

FERGUS

1. Templin Gardens
2. Post Office
3. "Kissing Stane"
4. St. Andrew's Church

FERGUS: LITTLE SCOTLAND

Fergus is on the Grand River where it intersects Highway 6. It is approximately twenty minutes north of Guelph and a hundred kilometres, or just over an hour's drive, from Toronto. It is only four kilometres upstream on the Grand from its arch-rival Elora. Like Elora, Fergus is favoured by excellent dam sites along the Grand River, but unlike Elora, Fergus owes much of its contemporary prosperity to industries stimulated by pioneering Scottish entrepreneurs. As a result of its early prosperity, the town boasts more excellent limestone buildings than any community of comparable size in Ontario. Over 200 such structures were built there during the nineteenth century by skilled Scottish stonemasons. The deep limestone gorge of the Grand River with its rapids and falls was crucial to the early development of mills and factories in Fergus.

THE FOUNDING OF FERGUS

Fergus was founded by the Honourable Adam Ferguson, a Scottish lawyer who was sent to Canada by the Highland Society

Left: *Melville United Church on the Grand River*

of Scotland to explore colonization possibilities. After visiting Niagara Falls, he journeyed to Guelph, where he was enthralled by the beauty and potential of the countryside. He returned to Scotland and persuaded fellow lawyer James Webster to emigrate to Canada with him. They arrived at the banks of the Grand River accompanied by six of Ferguson's seven sons in 1833. Armed with a deed and title to 7,300 acres they set out to build a settlement for "carefully selected Scottish immigrants who possessed money and education." According to Adam Ferguson, Fergus was to be a "centre of growth and activity" for Upper Canada.

In 1834, Ferguson constructed a primitive bridge across the river and within a year Fergus had a tavern, four streets and seventy inhabitants. Originally known as Little Falls, its name was changed to honour Adam Ferguson, who, along with James Webster, founded the community. The first mill was established where the Grand cascades over a falls just off St. Andrew Street. Its enterprising Scottish settlers worked hard to build a prosperous community.

When Ferguson left, two of his sons and Webster continued to promote the community, resuming Ferguson's

Templin Gardens

(1878) at the intersection of the Grand River and Highway 6. This business was founded to fabricate farm implements and in later years manufactured appliances, eventually succumbing to competition from more modern facilities in larger communities. In its limestone buildings beside the falls and rapids, vendors display their vegetables, potatoes, maple sugar candy and a wide array of collectibles. On Saturdays the buyers and sellers crowd the market. Patrons travel from Toronto, Kitchener and Guelph, as much to absorb the local colour as to bargain for antiques or crafts. The market's restaurant beside the river offers light meals and an unparalleled view of the rushing torrent below.

THE GORGE

The Grand River cascades over the dam built by Webster and Ferguson into a whirlpool called Mirror Basin, which has claimed the lives of several careless swimmers. The rugged limestone gorge is lined by a walkway and park, edging the swirl of frothing water with a riot of variegated colours. Templin Gardens, built in the late 1820s, descends to the river, creating a flowery oasis immediately behind St. Andrew Street. After falling into disrepair, the gardens were restored in the 1970s. A walkway along the gorge connects two downtown bridges. In the wall of the chasm below there are several caves, including the CPR Cave, named for a CPR lantern found there by intrepid speleologists. This was a favourite location for the manufacture of bootleg liquor.

In 1991 the Milligan pedestrian bridge was constructed from the market building to Templin Gardens. It provides excellent views of Melville United Church (1900), the rapids and Mirror Pool. Nearby was the site of the original "pig bridge" crossing the river. In the 1890s, after numerous complaints by local women about "nasty pigs" that were not penned and ran all over town, a narrow structure was built to link new pens to pastures south of the river. It took the roaming pigs off the streets and across their private bridge, much to the womens' relief. Eventually the bridge became a popular shortcut for pedestrians, despite its confined and slippery surface.

efforts to attract enterprising Scottish immigrants. By 1846, Fergus boasted twenty-one businesses, including a distillery, tannery and brewery in addition to shops and mills. In 1858, when its population reached 1,000, Fergus was incorporated as a village and functioned successfully as a mill town and rural service centre until the turn of the century. After 1900, its functions and population changed considerably, primarily because of the entrepreneurial initiative of Scottish settlers who promoted an increasing variety of industry.

ENTREPRENEURIAL INITIATIVES

The industrial sector of Fergus boasted several sawmills, distilleries, breweries, flax and woollen mills, tanneries, foundries and a stave factory. The Templin Carriage and Wagon Works began in 1869, while a sewing machine factory was one of the principal industries in the 1870s. In the early 1900s, Fergus attracted a wide variety of manufacturing and processing plants, providing local employment. Much of its later success as an industrial community and service centre resulted from vigorous local promotion.

Recently Fergus has been stimulated by entrepreneurs who have capitalized on its limestone legacy and river location. Its popular market occupies the former Beatty Brothers Foundry

The Breadalbane Inn

COMPETITION

Like many other Ontario service centres, Fergus felt the effects of improving technology and competition for trade. Larger settlements at Guelph and Kitchener became more attractive to settlers and industry. Between 1891 and 1911, Fergus lost twenty businesses, but its accessibility improved dramatically when a local politician had the Guelph-Fergus road designated a provincial highway and paved between 1922 and 1925. This increased accessibility contributed greatly to Fergus' growth as an industrial centre relying on motor transportation. After the Fergus road (now Highway 6) was paved, Fergus grew much more quickly than its nearby rival, Elora, which was left at the end of a gravel road leading nowhere.

LIMESTONE LEGACIES

Just across the river from the market on St. Andrew Street stand some of the finest examples of eclectic three-storey Victorian limestone architecture in Ontario. They endure as lasting monuments to the Scottish stonemasons who built the town. The post office (1911) at the corner of Tower and St. Andrew streets is a commemoration of the era when public buildings were symbols of civic pride. Its clock tower dominates the street. Across Tower Street to the west is the Breadalbane Inn (1870). This restored former residence of the founding Ferguson family is now an intimate, small hotel. Its original owner, George Ferguson, insisted on being called a gentleman

rather than the banker that he was. In those days, bankers were little respected as a group, and Ferguson, who was known for sharp practices, was less popular than most. Today the Breadalbane's superb dining room exudes old-world charm while its pub offers a wide variety of local and imported beers. The garden terrace and atrium are favourites for before and after theatre dining. Highly polished bannisters and wrought-iron rails recall an era of elegance and gentility that is rare in the modern world.

The magnificent churches on the St. Patrick Street hill, east of Breadalbane Street, are part of the same proud limestone tradition. Rivalry between Catholics and Protestants is reflected in their history. Ferguson and Webster set aside money for all denominations but decided that a swamp would do as a site for the Catholic church. The Catholic residents declined the suggested location and held out for the hill closer to the centre of town. St. Joseph's Roman Catholic Church was built in 1865, but lost its steeple in 1913 during a vicious winter storm. Without its tall steeple, it appears vaguely Norman, and is no longer an architectural challenge to the 1861 St. Andrew's Presbyterian Church nearby. St. Andrew's Church dominates the intersection of Tower and St. George streets, providing a magnificent vista to travellers from the south. Behind it lies the first burial ground of the village, the Auld Kirk Yard. Most early settlers were interred there, but neither Catholics nor the few local blacks were welcome. Originally Catholics were buried in plots near their church, but in the early 1900s, gravel was extracted from this location and later it became a dump. The

The post office, built in 1911

33

appearance of bones halted the gravel excavation, but left Catholics without a local cemetery. Catholic families often opted to bury their dead in Guelph, being prevented by civic rivalry and pride from using the cemetery in nearby Elora.

For those interested in municipal history, the old Council Chamber and Engine House is found at the north corner of Tower and St. Patrick streets. This simple, poorly-maintained structure was originally a two-storey building. Its austere architecture reflects the frugal attitudes of the original Scottish councillors. Nearby in James Square, the "kissing stane" lies under the trees. It was a favourite meeting spot for young people, who were allowed in Victorian times to kiss in public if sitting on the "stane."

ST. ANDREW STREET

A walk to the corner of St. Andrew Street and Provost Lane provides a contrast with the plain Council Chamber and Engine House. The commercial architecture created by early entrepreneurs was considerably more ornate, reflecting the prosperity of nineteenth-century Wellington County. East along St. Andrew Street, the tops of the buildings have date stones and all are historic. The reddish Marshall Block (1880) at the corner of St. David and St. Andrew streets is faced with Credit Valley sandstone, which was fashionable at the turn of the century. The Argo Block (1851–1855) across the street is one of the best examples of Ashlar limestone in Fergus. The front of the building of finely cut limestone was much more difficult and time-consuming to lay than the usual rubblestone sides and backs of local buildings. A peek behind most structures displays

St. Andrew's Presbyterian Church

the frugality and ingenuity of the Scottish settlers of Fergus.

The Theatre on the Grand at 244 St. Andrew Street opened as a movie house in 1928 and has endured a long struggle to remain a theatre. In 1991, citizens invested considerable sums to restore and operate it as a playhouse but finances became difficult. After much debate, Central Wellington Municipal Council purchased the property in 1999 and now leases it to the local professional theatre company. Supported by extensive fundraising activities, this year-round theatre continues to present outstanding productions. Works by several Canadian authors, including Margaret Atwood, have premiered there. Comfortable seats and exceptional sightlines are appreciated by the theatre-goers.

CONTEMPORARY CHARACTER

By 1970, Fergus had grown to 5,191 with sixty-four businesses

The "Kissing Stane"

and by 1981 its population was 6,065, while the number of businesses had burgeoned to 163. By 1996, 26 percent of Fergus workers were employed in retail, hospitality and service occupations. Some 30 percent of its employees worked in manufacturing, with significant percentages in clerical, business and finance categories. Fergus maintains its strong legacy of manufacturing and industry.

As its prosperous main street attests, Fergus remains an important local market town. Despite some modern improvements to shop fronts, St. Andrew Street would not be out of place in Scotland. Unfortunately, after several limestone blocks burned to the ground between 1940 and 1990, it was impossible to reconstruct them of stone. Prohibitive costs and the scarcity of stonemasons dictated modern replacements. On the north side of St. Andrew Street east of the modern Canada Trust building, the Russell Block and Commercial Hotel Building are excellent examples of meticulous stonework. After several renovations, both were faced with Credit Valley sandstone in the 1880s. The former Egg Emporium lies to the south, from 216 to 224 St. Andrew Street. Here eggs were sorted, pickled and stored. Its facade has changed little over the years, but it is now occupied by the Copper Kettle Restaurant and Pub, and by Kitchens to Go catering. The interior of James Russell and Sons across the street remains much as it was from the beginning.

At the eastern extremity of the river through town, the massive well-preserved Monkland mills rise majestically above the river, overlooking their line of dams. On a fine July day, groups of artists painting and sketching become part of the scene. By the dam, several anglers fish for brown trout in what has become one of the best trout streams in North America. The mills are a reminder of the prominent importance of wheat and water, stream and dam to the economy of early Ontario. These solid buildings from 1835, now empty, invite some modern use, be it incubator for industry or studio for arts and crafts. The latest scheme is to create condominiums to sell from $150,000 to over $300,000. The time and location appear to be ripe for retirees and those seeking a tranquil escape from the city.

Fergus celebrates its Scottish heritage by hosting Highland Games on the second full weekend of August. The games began as a one-day event with 300 participants in 1946, but now attract competitors from all over the world. A host of Scottish competitions include highland dancing, piping contests, the hammer throw and caber toss. Each year, over 30,000 people attend the Games, which feature an outdoor tattoo (Scottish musical event) and other musical attractions. For several days a year, Fergus returns to its Scottish roots with a vengeance. Streets are festooned with Scottish flags while banners and kilts appear everywhere in the town.

Today Fergus is a thriving service centre with diversified industry, growing modern residential suburbs and a rich history. Efforts have been made to capitalize on its superb site and historic limestone buildings. Many of its splendid homes have plaques listing the names of original owners and their occupations. Styles range from plain Ontario cottages to ornate Victorian mansions. Fergus offers good accommodation in the Breadalbane and several bed and breakfasts. The citizens are friendly and the ambience is pleasant. It provides a hospital, facilities for the elderly and excellent access to Toronto and the Golden Triangle. Despite its strong industrial legacy, the atmosphere remains that of a bustling market town on the river. Its economic prospects and tourist potential are great, as is its future as a growing residential community.

Monkland Mills

MEAFORD

Georgian Bay

1. Starting point of Georgian Trail
2. Rotary Harbour Pavillion
3. Fire Hall
4. Town Hall & Opera House
5. Meaford Museum

Memorial Park

Cemetery

Grant Ave.

Aiken St.

Georgian Trail

Harbour

Boucher St.

St. Vincent St.

26

7

Inner Harbour

Bayfield

Sykes St.

Victoria Cres.

Beautiful Joe Park

Sykes St.

26

Parker

Collingwood St.

Nelson St.

Trowbridge St.

County

Golf Course

12

Bighead River

MEAFORD: HARBOUR TOWN

Meaford lies at the mouth of the Bighead River on the shore of Nottawasaga Bay thirteen kilometres west of Thornbury. The site of Meaford is a sloping bench created by the waters of the retreating lake Nipissing at the end of the Wisconsin Glacial Period. Today the town spreads across this ridge and slopes to the water. According to an early immigrant, this created "a view from the deck of a steamer of a busy little town nestling at the foot of a gently inclining background, in which the beauties of rural scenery are liberally displayed, which is remarkably pleasant and exhilarating."

The Bighead River occupies a major pre-glacial notch through the Lockport Dolomite of the Niagara Escarpment. It rushes along a wide valley leading to gently rolling hills inland from Meaford. The glacial legacy of the Pleistocene has contributed immensely to local scenery, just as the towering escarpment provides breathtaking viewpoints over Meaford and Nottawasaga Bay.

The area between the Niagara Escarpment and

Left: *The town hall and opera house*

Nottawasaga Bay has a unique microclimate because of the warming effects of the water and the shelter provided by the uplands to the south. It has always been particularly suited to the production of fruit, especially apples, plums and pears. Fruit farming began early here, declined in the 1970s and 1980s, but recently has become important again. Its unique local physiography has had a major effect on the economy of this whole area.

INITIAL SURVEY AND SETTLEMENT

Meaford was surveyed and settled around the same time as Thornbury, but grew more quickly and to a larger size. Charles Rankin, who also laid out Thornbury's town plot, surveyed St. Vincent Township where Meaford was founded in 1838. The first settler was David Miller, from Ireland, who built a cabin two years later on the banks of the Bighead and started a community. Since Miller's shanty was the disembarkation point for early settlers arriving by bateaux, the location was named Peggy's Landing after his wife. The little settlement grew on the two hundred acres left for the town plot, which was covered by a tangled mass of cedar and brush down to the rocky shores. In the early years it was the entry point for everyone coming to Sydenham (now Owen Sound) and the surrounding area, attracting numerous settlers who brought much-needed business to the local economy.

Miller's son, David, was the first to use power provided by the river when he constructed a mill in 1840. It ultimately failed because of his inexperience as a millwright. The property was eventually purchased and operated by Jesse T. Purdy, who became a prominent local businessman. William Stephenson arrived from Yorkshire around the same time to build the Georgian Inn, which was the first hotel and tavern in the district. Nearby, a small wharf was constructed to receive settlers and the early-trading vessels that called at the harbour. Before the railway, people and goods either arrived by water or through dense mosquito-and-blackfly-infested bush. In the spring and fall, trails became muddy quagmires, while in summer they were all but impenetrable. Little wonder that canoes were the preferred mode of travel.

Soon after 1840, Stephenson became postmaster and mail carrier from Barrie, a trip he often made on foot along rough trails. His tavern served as both a local gathering place and post office until he died in 1858. On Saturday nights the millpond was thronged with canoes carrying settlers from the east bank of the river to collect their mail, drink in the tavern and shop in town. In 1844, Moses Chantler came to the community and constructed a mill, which was destroyed by fire. His important legacy was the first bridge across the river, which he erected in 1847.

In 1845, Meaford proper was born as W. R. Gibbard, the provincial land surveyor, completed the layout of the town plot. He called the settlement Meaford after the country estate in Staffordshire owned by Sir John Jervis, Earl of St. Vincent, after whom St. Vincent township had been named. Streets such as Collingwood, Parker, Nelson and Trowbridge honoured famous British admirals and statesmen. Growth was slow until 1850, when the settlement had only ten houses. It accelerated when Purdy surveyed his land south of the village and encouraged settlers to build in what became known as Purdytown. Meanwhile, Stephenson was promoting his land to the north, creating two separate rival hamlets.

CATASTROPHES AND NATURAL DISASTERS

As farmers began to clear the densely forested hinterland of Meaford, water that had been held in check by the trees and underbrush ran off too quickly in the spring. Instead of seeping slowly into the ground, it rushed in increasingly large freshets to the river, which could not contain the torrent. As it tumbled downstream, flood water spilled from the banks, inundating farms and structures in the village. Numerous floods destroyed buildings too close to the river and covered streets with silt and mud. The "big flood" occurred in 1912, when the power dam, bridge, flour mill, tannery, railway embankment and some houses were swept away by the foaming deluge.

Since wooden buildings were common, fires occurred frequently. The most memorable took place in 1913 when a grain elevator in the harbour was destroyed. For a time the whole town was threatened, as flames driven by howling winds off the lake crept inexorably inland. Fortunately, the conflagration burnt out before reaching the settlement. Ultimately, wood was replaced by brick and flood-control measures were adopted, greatly decreasing the frequency of such disasters.

GROWTH AND INCORPORATION

Unlike other Ontario communities, Meaford bypassed the normal incorporation procedure. In 1874, with its population at 1,700, too low for incorporation under the General Act, Meaford was incorporated under a special act of the Ontario

Park on Bayfield Street

Stucco home and garden

legislature. Subsequently, growth accelerated as the port became a major grain (wheat) exporting facility and the terminus of the Northern Railway. Council and local merchants offered the line incentives to extend its tracks from Collingwood, which it had reached in 1885.

THE OLD HARBOUR

By the turn of the century, the harbour at the mouth of the river, now the old harbour, was used regularly by passenger boats, tugs, dredgers, fishing boats, steamers and freighters carrying lumber, coal and grain. It was served by an enormous grain elevator and railway station and protected by a wooden breakwater and lighthouse. Its role as a major port contributed substantially to Meaford's growth. By 1952 the town had reached 3,169, growing steadily to 4,520 in 1991 and to 4,681 by 1996.

For years Meaford continued to be an important terminal for lake freighters and a centre of shipbuilding. Bayfield Street follows the old harbour along the east side of the river, just a block north of the historic fire hall and Town Hall, providing easy access to its many attractions. Cliff Richardson's boat works in this harbour began building wooden fishing vessels in the 1930s, followed by life boats for the Canadian navy during the Second World War. Today Richardson's continues to manufacture pleasure craft and work boats. Off season their two large

lifts are used to take vessels out of the water for storage or repair. Their facilities accommodate almost 200 boats.

Unlike the old harbour, which is shallow in places and difficult to navigate, the recently constructed small-craft harbour east of the river is deep and safe. It has slips for 200 boats, a double-width boat launch and pump-out facilities for waste. Slips may now be reserved by marine radio, and users have access to shower and washroom facilities. The red-and-white coast guard ships at their search-and-rescue base add colour to this modern facility with its beautifully landscaped breakwater wall. *The Spume*, the last wooden coast guard cutter to be built on Georgian Bay, reminds visitors of former boat-building activities. It was built in Penetanguishene in 1963 and was stationed in Meaford for fifteen years, with the remainder of its time at Port Dover. At 21 metres in length and with 1,050 horsepower, *The Spume* was a formidable asset to the Canadian Coast Guard. Since 1994 the vessel has stood proudly beside the new small-craft marina.

Today the waterfront is a major recreational area adorned by parks and the Meaford Museum. Several pleasant restaurants by the old harbour feature seafood, while the new marina provides full services and fishing charters. Its modern building at the foot of St. Vincent Street contains the dock master's office, lounges and meeting rooms for boaters. Cobblestone paths flank the old harbour, linking it to parks and fishing areas to the west and to the business area and river to the east. Both harbours are within easy walking distance of the town's thriving downtown.

Meaford's busy commercial harbour of long ago has been replaced by the beautiful, new recreational boating facility. The Bighead remains one of the best trout and salmon streams in Ontario, attracting anglers year round. The harbours are used heavily in the summer by boaters, sailors and anglers, who store their craft there in the winter. The old harbour has retained many of its heritage characteristics and is a pleasant environment with splendid views at all times of year. Landscaped paths surround both old and new harbours while both adjoin some of the prettiest residential neighbourhoods in town.

HISTORIC BUILDINGS AND ATTRACTIONS

Contemporary Meaford continues as a rural service centre and port, but is increasingly becoming a vacation destination. The Tourist Apple near the corner of Sykes and Collingwood streets is an excellent location to start a walk around town. Here

Meaford's Fire Hall

friendly senior volunteers provide maps, tourist literature and a wealth of useful advice.

Directly east of the Apple stands the Town Hall Opera House. Built in 1903, it was one of Ontario's original opera houses, now home to the Georgian Theatre Festival. For the last five years the theatre has presented all-Canadian musical and theatrical events in its beautifully restored facility. This handsome three-storey structure of red brick personifies Meaford's importance at the turn of the century before the motor vehicle diminished its stature. Fortuitously, it avoided the fate of so many similar structures demolished in the name of "progress" in the 50s and 60s.

Meaford's Romanesque-revival fire hall, just north of the opera house on Nelson Street, stands tall beside the former mill close to the water. Its tower reaches to the sky, the summit topped by a bell. The loop along Bayfield Street passes a former mill and a quaint clapboard structure now serving as a bookstore. Across the street, Richardson's Boat Works beside the Meaford Museum continues to repair sailing craft.

The Meaford Museum occupies the town's original pump house, which was built in 1895. Its Victorian exterior has decorated eaves consistent with its status as an important working facility at the turn of the century. It now houses a collection of marine and farm exhibits, period costumes and a 1938 Bickle Maple Leaf fire truck. Scarecrows in its garden add a festive touch during the spectacular days of autumn.

A stroll from the old harbour to the corner of Bayfield and Sykes streets leads to delightful lakeside plantings and views. From there heading east, Sykes Street displays some of the most interesting architecture from the turn of the century. Three-storey businesses of local, 1870s soft salmon brick alternate with more recent buildings of glazed red brick. Intricate patterns adorn the upper stories of what is now Stedmans, while a lifelike picture depicts Paul's Hotel at the corner of Sykes and Trowbridge streets. Both sides of Sykes between Parker and Trowbridge are lined by some of the best-preserved Victorian business blocks and houses in the area.

CHURCH WINDOWS

Christchurch Anglican Church on Boucher Street just north of Highway 26, exhibits the results of the Second World War as well as some important British heritage. Its pastor then, Reverend Harold Appleyard, arrived in England with the Canadian Fusiliers in 1942. Everywhere he travelled he witnessed the devastation wrought by German bombs. Most disturbing were the shards of stained glass remaining after cathedral windows had been shattered. Soon he was spending every spare moment gathering, cleaning, identifying and labelling remnants of windows from bombed churches across Britain.

Before returning to Canada, he scrounged a metal artillery chest in which to store the fragments and asked a window-maker to create a design from the glass that would fit windows in Christchurch. Today six windows in the church display the rich colours rescued from British cathedrals, including those at Canterbury, Chichester, Manchester and Brighton. These historic, artistic creations have received publicity in the *Canadian Geographic* magazine and *Reader's Digest*. The public is welcome to view them when the church is open, or on arranged guided tours.

The Apple

BEAUTIFUL JOE

In 1894, Margaret Marshall Saunders came to Meaford from Nova Scotia to visit her in-laws, the Moores, who had recently nursed an abused dog back to health. They had rescued it from a cruel owner who had beaten it and cut off its tail and ears. The incident inspired Ms. Saunders to write an autobiographical account of the dog's ordeal entitled *Beautiful Joe*. The book won a contest sponsored by the American Humane and Educational Society, which was seeking a sequel to *Black Beauty*. Because female authors were not popular at the time, Saunders entered the contest under her middle name of Marshall and won.

Published in 1893, *Beautiful Joe* was chosen as one of Canada's ten best children's books, became the first Canadian book to sell over a million copies and was translated into fourteen languages. It remains an icon for those opposing cruelty to animals. Joe's burial plot is in Beautiful Joe Park by the river and Victoria Crescent. Saunders' legacy is now honoured by the Beautiful Joe Heritage Society, a charitable foundation dedicated to animal welfare. The book continues to be popular.

JOHN MUIR

The Meaford Museum prides itself on its collection of letters written by John Muir, founder of the Sierra Club. He came to Meaford in 1864 from Scotland via Wisconsin and lived in the village for two years. His major contribution was to spearhead the environmental and conservation movement.

Muir worked in the Trout Mill, established on the Bighead River in 1856 by William Trout. The mill thrived at first, but the worldwide depression made it unprofitable. Trout and his sons then used the water power to run their small-implement factory, aided considerably by Muir's mechanical talents. The factory prospered for a time and was also used as a base for Muir's botanical expeditions. Unfortunately, on February 21,1866, it burned to the ground, ending an important period in the history of Meaford. Not only did the business cease, but Muir moved on, never to return. He continues to be commemorated by symposia and walking tours in the area.

One tour honouring Muir includes the former tank range, 6,880 hectares of uncultivated land west off Highway 26, that is home to many mammals, reptiles and birds. This relatively untouched area displays numerous original animal inhabitants of the area, including hare, beaver, porcupine, weasel, deer, turtles,

The Meaford Museum

tree frogs and 142 species of birds. It is a living museum — a fitting, although inadvertent tribute to Muir's conservation contributions. The area was originally reserved for the Canadian Forces to hold manoeuvres and practice live firing.

Meaford combines the best qualities of fishing port and quiet residential community. The old harbour reflects a past of boat building and lake traders, while the new harbour caters to pleasure craft and anglers. Sykes Street provides a wide variety of shopping and boasts some lovely brick buildings. The Town Hall Opera House offers year-round theatre and concerts, while the excellent Meaford Museum illuminates the past. But the town's most appealing characteristic is the long, lovely waterfront with its gracious homes, carefully manicured parks and quiet ambience. It has not been spoiled by commercialization or over-development.

Christchurch Anglican Church

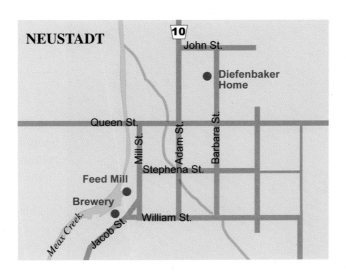

NEUSTADT: BEER, SPRINGS AND CAVERNS

The German community of Neustadt (literally, new town) lies on a gently rolling plain along the Grey-Bruce County boundary about halfway between Hanover and Clifford. Its site near the Saugeen River on the Meaux (or Meax) Creek provided both power for a mill and potable water. In a secluded limestone cavern beside the creek, settlers found a spring of clear, pure water. The spring, and the falls where a dam was created, became the foundation for Neustadt's most important industries, and much later helped to rejuvenate the village.

SETTLEMENT AND EARLY DEVELOPMENT

In 1855, David Winkler came to Normanby Township and squatted on four hundred acres of land near the junction of the Saugeen River and the Meaux Creek. The following year, he purchased the land at the present site of Neustadt and founded the settlement. The Saugeen River flows about a kilometre east of the village, and it first appeared that the village would be established there at Viel-Noethig, which means "much needed" in German. By 1856, a woollen mill, gristmill, hotel and flax mill were located there, but they soon were replaced by others

Left: *St. Paul's – Normanby Lutheran Church*

on the nearby Meaux Creek. Despite the fact that the creek was a small tributary of the Saugeen, it offered a better dam site with a greater drop and steeper banks. Soon the dam had been constructed and the present millpond appeared. A bonus for the Meaux site was the spring for drinking water and the limestone caverns.

In 1857, David Winkler dammed the Meaux and erected a sawmill, gristmill and flour mill. They were successful and became the economic basis for Neustadt. By 1865 Neustadt had 300 residents and was growing rapidly. Although a flax mill remained at Viel-Noethig, less than a kilometre away, the other functions established at Neustadt continued to thrive and attracted increasing business and population. It, rather than Viel-Noethig, became the major settlement in the area.

GROWTH

A major addition to the village was the brewery, built in 1859 by Henry Heuther, a German immigrant to Neustadt. He selected a site next to the millpond over the caverns beside the mill. Wishing to adhere to the Bavarian Purity Laws of 1516, Heuther used the clear, pure water from Crystal Springs below. His products immediately became popular in the village and

A Victorian cottage

and processing flax was an important local enterprise, especially in Normanby Township. During "pulling season" (harvest) it employed many local children who worked for the farmers. The local mill did not produce linen, but "scutched" the flax and bundled it for additional processing. "Scutching" consisted of crushing threshed flax with a "breaker," which was a heavy sharp-ribbed iron roller. Then a roughing and finishing process prepared the product for baling and shipping to Doon, near Kitchener, where it was spun, woven and bleached for heavy fabrics.

The flax mill provided incentives to local farmers to grow its raw material. If the company supplied the seed, farmers were required to return an equal amount of seed in the fall. Or they could have the value of the seed deducted from their payment from the mill. In 1864, the straw, which was pulled and dried in the fields with the seeds on, was worth about $10 a ton. If a farmer threshed the flax himself, he received half, which he might either spin or sell to the company at ten cents a pound. A few years later, most farmers threshed their crop and sold seed to the mill for $1.12 a bushel. Others rented land to the mill at $5 an acre. This arrangement required the farmers to plough in and harrow the seeds. For a few years, the flax mill brought considerable prosperity to the area as a cash crop for farmers and as a source of seasonal employment for school children.

In the 1870s, the community boasted four thriving churches, which served its large rural hinterland. German was the language of choice for most services as traditions from the homeland were preserved. Rivalry was strong, especially between Protestants and Catholics and also between Baptists and Lutherans. By 1872 each of these denominations and the Evangelicals had erected fine church buildings. In 1880 a branch line of the Grand Trunk Railway arrived in Neustadt, making it a convenient shipping point for farm produce, which now included beef and wheat. Pubs in four hotels thrived as the population reached 466 in 1901. The first of two furniture factories was built in 1904.

surrounding area, bringing business and a reputation for fine German beer to the settlement.

Heuther was one of many early settlers who transformed Neustadt into a community with strong German traditions, one where German is spoken today. Along with his brewery, Heuther also began a boot-making and shoemaking business to diversify his enterprises. About the same time, John Weinart built a tannery. Soon the community grew to support three stores, three hotels, two blacksmiths, a school and a large frame Roman Catholic Church. A woollen mill and foundry were also established by the early 1860s.

PEAK OF PROSPERITY

By the turn of the century, Neustadt was firmly established as the local service centre, especially for the German farmers who had settled in southern Bruce County. They came to have grain ground, to purchase supplies and to use the post office. Of course, a draught of fine German Pilsner in the pub was always welcome. The village's founder, David Winkler, functioned as postmaster from 1857 until 1880.

Just a short distance away at Viel-Noethig, Messrs. Perene and Hendry employed about fifteen hands in their new flax mill, which opened in 1864. For a number of years, growing

Although Neustadt's population dropped to a low of 419 in 1941, it remained relatively steady around 450 through the thirties when other centres were suffering because of increased competition brought about by motor transport. Neustadt's core of local services continued to attract loyal German farmers from its hinterland, as the flour and chopping mill, then powered by electricity, and the one remaining hotel continued to function. A hardware store and farm supply outlet were added attractions. Strong loyalty to their churches and to Neustadt kept the German-speaking customers coming to the community.

The brewery

THE MILL

Three important buildings from the 1800s remain to contribute character and economic stimulation to Neustadt. Winkler's flour mill rose to three stories, the lower storey constructed of local fieldstone. It boasted two sets of stones and was supplied with water power by the same dam that served the sawmill. Despite turbulent economic times, it continued as a mill until recently, when it was converted into an antique store that also sells foods and crafts produced by Mennonite farmers. Delicious summer sausages, homemade pastries and handmade clothing are available from young women wearing traditional black Mennonite clothing and head coverings. Much of the mill has been restored to its original condition, and its machinery is on display in the basement. Those visiting the mill can peer into the caverns, which will soon be opened for tours.

The mill

THE BREWERY

The brewery occupied a splendid fieldstone building of two stories on the pond just upstream from the mill. It produced fine German Pilsner beer under Henry and then his son William Heuther until it was closed by Prohibition and declining local population in 1916. For a time the building functioned as a creamery and a scheme was later developed to convert it into a retirement home. This never occurred, and the solid structure remained

Neustadt Tavern

empty until the Stimpson family reopened the brewery. After it had lain dormant for eighty-one years, production began again in 1997, once again using water from Crystal Springs and following the Bavarian Purity Laws of 1516. Heuther's Brewery was reborn as Neustadt Springs Brewery.

Today Neustadt Heavy Ale is brewed in a traditional Scottish style. It is deep golden in colour and full-bodied. Neustadt Lager Beer is brewed in the Belgian country style and is somewhat more full-bodied than the traditional Canadian lager. Both are available at the brewery and across much of Southwestern Ontario. A new beer called "Lale" (lager and ale mixed) has been introduced, as has local cheese containing Neustadt beer. Also available are a number of local beef and vegetable products either marinated or cooked in Neustadt beer. Tours take visitors through the brewery and the caverns.

THE TAVERN

The third historic structure, also of distinctive local fieldstone crafted carefully by skilled German masons is the former Commercial Hotel, now the Neustadt Tavern. It is at the corner of Stephana and Mill streets and was built a year before the survey in 1858. This architectural gem has metre-thick stone walls and displays superb craftsmanship. During Prohibition, it relied on room rental to survive, but continued as a hotel. It now offers a bar and country dining to its patrons. The motor car and lack of business eventually reduced Neustadt's five hotels of the 1870s to this sole survivor, even though the local population remained relatively stable.

The tavern even has a friendly ghost. The story goes that over fifty years ago, George, a local gentleman farmer, dropped by to quench his thirst after supervising haying on his farm.

Shop on Queen Street

Dropping by the "local" was then both a business and social occasion. Workers were often either paid or hired in the pub, while travelling salesmen displayed and sold their wares. The front room doubled as lounge and waiting area for stage coach travellers.

George, tired and slightly inebriated, stumbled on the way to the basement washroom. Unfortunately, he fell and broke his neck. Death was instant and George has never left the tavern. Even today, doors open by themselves, the jukebox begins to play at four a.m. and light bulbs frequently and mysteriously burn out. "George" seems harmless, but tavern proprietors tire of changing as many as five light bulbs in three days, especially when three are from the same lamp. Today all washrooms are on the main floor, and George has joined the ranks of ghosts in old Ontario buildings.

POPULATION AND EMPLOYMENT

From a low of 419 in 1941, Neustadt's population increased slowly, reaching 579 in 1961 and has remained roughly the same since then. No major periods of rapid growth or recession have affected the village during the last fifty years. Unlike some of the other communities, there are no large new subdivisions in Neustadt and its businesses are relatively stable. Here and there new homes are built on vacant land, while a few others change hands. Employment is relatively diversified among local sales and service jobs and trades. The brewery provides steady jobs, as do several local construction companies that build for local farmers and in Hanover and Clifford.

There are proportionately fewer working in recreational enterprises than in other small towns and villages, but the main street is becoming more tourist-oriented as the village begins to be "discovered."

OTHER ATTRACTIONS

Just a block off Main Street, comfortable homes on large treed lots invite new arrivals seeking a quiet country haven. John Diefenbaker, Prime Minister of Canada from June 1957 to April 1963, was born in a modest home on Barbara Street on September 18, 1895. The building, which had begun to deteriorate, has now been purchased and is being renovated as an historic site. It will eventually be opened to the public as a tourist attraction.

Neustadt is a delightful village, populated by numerous descendants of its original German settlers. Its brewery and hotel continue to reflect their early influence. It boasts large green yards, a pretty stream and friendly people. Its setting in the Meaux Valley is compact and picturesque. A retirement home is available for seniors, and most essential goods are obtainable locally. Neustadt is the quintessential "quiet rural residential village by a stream." The village and its bucolic rural hinterland are well worth a visit for a day.

A Victorian house in town

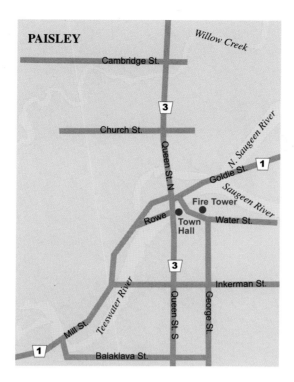

PAISLEY: BRIDGE TOWN

Paisley is a village of rivers and bridges. Situated at the confluence of the Saugeen and Teeswater rivers, close to Willow Creek and the North Saugeen, it has long depended on its streams for power, transportation, and more recently, for business. The community lies in its "quadruple valley" in the midst of rolling moraine and till plain in the heart of Bruce County, now a major beef-producing area of Ontario. Historically it has served as a market centre and shipping point for its rich agricultural hinterland.

DISCOVERY AND SETTLEMENT
Before the 1850s, the confluence of the Teeswater and Saugeen rivers remained an isolated tract in the midst of dense bush and undergrowth. In the winter of 1850/51, a man named Simon Orchard decided to move from Walkerton, some fifteen miles

Left: Town Hall, built in 1876

south, and pioneer a new settlement. That spring, he built a raft of cedar logs, loaded his family and possessions, and floated down the Saugeen River in search of a new homestead. Their first night's stop was at the rapids where the Saugeen and Teeswater meet, a location that they liked immediately and where they decided to stay.

Three weeks after the Orchards arrived, Simon's brother-in-law, Samuel Rowe, built two large rafts and followed Simon's route. He and his family settled on the south bank of the Teeswater River, directly across from the Orchards. Life was difficult during the first few years, because there was nothing to feed the cattle brought by the pioneers. That winter, snow lay one and a half metres deep in the woods, remaining well into June in the swamps. The settlers hired two men to fell trees so their tops could be fed to their cattle. Having survived the winter, Rowe's four cows came to the river to drink in the spring, but fell through rotten ice, never to be seen again.

Queen Street North

The initial development of Paisley proceeded quickly. Having lived in a shanty during the first season, Rowe hired men who cut logs and helped him to build Rowe's Tavern opposite the present Town Hall. It was ten by eight metres, with a lean-to for a kitchen and dining room. A major inconvenience was the separation of the Orchards and Rowes by the Teeswater River. In the winter they could sometimes cross on the ice, but the warmer weather posed major problems. An innovative solution for a time was the use of a dog trained to swim across the river, carrying small items from one shanty to the other. Finally they built a footbridge, which was washed away by the spring floods (called "freshets" in those days) in 1853.

By 1853 a newcomer, John Valentine, had applied for and taken possession of the mill site on the Teeswater. Before the mill was built, one of his men died and lumber was so scarce that planks from the floor of Rowe's house had to be used to build the coffin. By the end of the year, the sawmill was operating, supplying much-needed lumber to settlers along the rivers. The more versatile lumber, which was floated or rafted, quickly replaced logs as the primary building material.

The founders of Paisley remained squatters for many years. Despite paying the required fees to the Crown Land Agent and visiting the Crown Land Department at Quebec and Toronto, Orchard and Rowe could not obtain Crown patents for their land. Some believed that those in power had seen the site's potential and were attempting through their political connections to hold the land for speculation. Finally, in 1856, the provincial land surveyor, Frances Kerr, made the survey. Title to the large number of village and park lots was then officially conveyed to Rowe and Orchard.

TRANSPORTATION AND THE RIVER
The rivers were a mixed blessing. On the one hand, they provided a link to the outside world via Walkerton and

Southampton. On the other hand, they were difficult to cross and flooded each spring. After the original footbridge had been washed away, serious attempts were made to provide secure crossings of both rivers. A wooden bridge over the Saugeen was under construction during the period when settlers were going to Southampton for the "Big Land Sale" in 1854. Simon Orchard built the Goldie Street bridge in 1859. Later all early bridges were replaced with steel structures. A two-lane bridge over the Teeswater was opened in 1895, with Rae's new bridge opening in 1893 and the new Goldie Street bridge in 1891.

Spring floods increased in volume as the land was cleared. Before the bridge across the Saugeen was completed, scows transported people and goods across the stream for up to six days in the spring. So much harm was done by freshets that every house north of the Teeswater had its foundation raised to avoid flood damage. But the rivers were useful even after the coming of the railway. In the summer of 1879, a local resident, D. Hanna, built a flat-bottomed steamer called the Waterwitch. For several years thereafter this six-horsepower vessel carried travellers to and from Walkerton during Fall Fair celebrations. It took thirteen hours to go up the river, but could return in four. It did a roaring business as everyone wanted to try the little steamer. In 1883 it was sold and taken by sleigh to Boat Lake, where it continued to sail for a number of years. Surprisingly, the Saugeen was never dammed, although the Teeswater was harnessed in two locations. This may be one reason why Paisley never developed a major industrial base.

PAISLEY IN 1856

By 1856, the community was growing rapidly and the first important buildings had been constructed. Most of the thirty-six structures were scattered along Queen Street and down Alma to Valentine's Mill. The village plan showed three sawmills, a gristmill, a school and Rowe's Tavern as well as a number of houses. It indicated no bridges over either the Saugeen River or Willow Creek. In 1856, the post office was established at the same time as the mail route from Elora to Southampton. Initially, mail was delivered three times a week. Thomas Orchard became the first postmaster and the village was named Paisley, after a town near Glasgow, Scotland. Earlier in 1854, Orchard had also become the first merchant, doing business from a room in Rowe's tavern. He then built his own

store, which eventually became Robert Scott's flour and feed store.

Tradesmen began to come to Paisley as the hinterland filled with farmers. Thomas Irving personified the early jack-of-all-trades. His little workroom in Starke's Mill was everything from a foundry to a watchmaker's shop. There, Irving repaired many things from guns to printing presses, clocks and watches. Soon a sash and door factory, a tannery, a blacksmith shop and a brickyard had been established. By 1859, St.

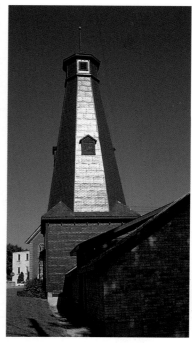

The fire tower

Andrew's Presbyterian Church was founded and Sergison's Hotel offered a cosy bar, heated by a wide brick fireplace piled with cherry logs. After a long cold sleigh ride from Kincardine, it offered warmth both inside and out, as the whiskey flowed freely to its patrons. Like other early hotels it is long gone.

GROWTH AND INCORPORATION

Communications improved considerably when the Montreal Telegraph Company established an office in 1869. For twenty years after its first settlement, the principal route between Paisley and the outside world had been by boat via Southampton and then by steamer to Goderich. In the winter it was necessary to travel overland eighty miles to the railway in Guelph.

After years of poor access, villagers cheered when the Wellington, Grey and Bruce Railway opened in August 1872. Instead of being a way station for sleighs passing through to Southampton, Paisley became a destination for produce heading to market by rail. Farmers began to bring their wheat and cattle to the village and then stayed to drink, eat, collect mail and purchase their supplies. The local economy benefited immensely from this trade. During this booming period, Paisley boasted five hotels.

By 1873, the population stood at 1,038, enough to achieve incorporation, which was granted on June 7 of that year. In the fall of 1876, the present Town Hall was built and the first council meeting was held there on March 20, 1877. Ten years later, the village installed its first water works at a cost of $6,500, greatly reducing the premiums for local fire insurance. Previously, the town had incurred serious losses through fires. Since 1871, both Stark's gristmill and Murdoch's woollen mill had burned to the ground.

Several banks have been located in the village, but only the Royal remains. In 1877 Robert Porteous opened a private bank, which he operated with Edward Saunders until Porteous died in 1896. By 1907 there were two sawmills, two gristmills, a cider mill and a creamery, but only one hotel, the Paisley Inn, survived. A number of small factories came and went, but a major enterprise, Bruce Packers, was established on the outskirts of town and continues to be important to the local economy.

In 1923, $16,000 in local debentures were issued to bring electric power. In 1935, two new bridges were built with county help, one on Willow Street and one on Queen Street. By 1939 additional debentures were issued to pave side streets and build the Cambridge Street bridge. During and after the 1930s, growth in Paisley slowed and became almost stagnant as the population sunk to around 700 for many years. Motor transportation and competition from larger places had taken their toll. Disaster struck when a new arena built in 1948 burned to the ground five days after it was opened. Gifts and hard work led to the building of another in 1949. After the end of the Second World War, a modern water and fire protection system was installed, and in 1952, new water filtration was added.

Bruce County has always been renowned for its beef production, which has contributed greatly to the economy of

The former Paisley Inn

Paisley. After the advent of cars, trucks and paved roads, Paisley lost some local business, but continued to ship beef to market. In 1967 some 1,200 yearling Hereford cattle were trucked from Paisley to feedlots in Chatham. Now much of this business goes to Bruce Packers, which produces specialty sausages as well as fine cuts of meat for merchants across the province. The hinterlands of Paisley continue to be among the major beef producers in Ontario.

CONTEMPORARY CHARACTER

With a population of only 720 in 1968, Paisley began to grow again as its functions slowly changed. The same motor transport that threatened its existence as a service centre made it accessible to commuters and retirees. The rivers that figured so prominently in its history took on a new life as recreational waterways. Fishing, hiking and canoeing replaced milling as the major functions of the Teeswater and Saugeen rivers. The Saugeen River offers ninety-seven kilometres of canoeing or kayaking without any portages. Sports outfitters and boat

Soapmaking in the 1890 Steele Block

tecture. In some ways, Paisley is just another sleepy little Ontario village, but in others it is unique. Its lovely parks, six bridges and historic Town Hall complement its pleasant residential areas and fire tower.

Paisley has become a centre for campers, anglers, kayakers and canoeists. A large proportion of its residents are now employed in outfitting, artistic occupations and retail sales. The town has changed considerably from its origins as a milling, manufacturing and rural service centre to cater today to visitors and an increasing number of retirees seeking a pleasant country lifestyle. By 1981, Paisley had equalled its earlier high with 1,038 inhabitants, increasing to 1,106 in

rentals have become as important as land and inexpensive real estate as engines of growth in the village.

Today Paisley remains an important rural service centre, as Bruce Packers continues to process and export meat products for farmers from Bruce and Grey counties. But more obvious to today's visitors are its recreational facilities. Shops and restaurants serving the hinterland have been augmented by those catering to the tourist trade. Soap-making and gold-smithing are now carried out in the village. An excellent local museum, lapidary art studio and specialty bakeries serve visitors and residents alike. The village's campground along the Saugeen provides a pleasant alternative to its bed and breakfasts. The Saugeen Bluffs Conservation Area is just a few kilometres from the settlement.

Flooding in Paisley has finally been tamed by one of the largest dyking projects in Ontario. Walking paths follow several of the dykes, and in the autumn, salmon may be seen swimming up the river or leaping over the old dam at the Fisher Mill as they head to their spawning grounds. The village offers a local Architectural Conservancy walking tour of its interesting historic archi-

1996 and projected to reach 1,319 by 2011. Much of the anticipated growth is expected to be from farmers retiring to their former service centre, and from city dwellers moving to the country for a change in lifestyle.

Dam on the Teeswater River

53

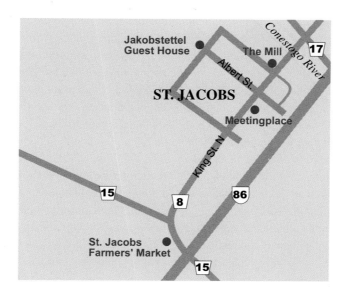

St. Jacobs: Mennonite Heritage

St. Jacobs lies in the middle of one of the most productive and historic areas of Ontario. Situated between Waterloo and Elmira and surrounded by fertile rolling hills, it is nestled in the valley of the Conestogo River, which flows in a broad glacial spillway. In 1805, frugal, efficient, Mennonite farmers from Lancaster County, Pennsylvania, came to settle Waterloo County. They quickly transformed this virgin territory into a rich and productive agricultural hinterland for St. Jacobs and Berlin (later named Kitchener). Today St. Jacobs is a bustling community with Mennonite shops and markets attracting visitors from across the country. Its transition from a rural service centre to a thriving tourist town had its origins in the middle 1800s.

THE FOUNDING OF ST. JACOBS

St. Jacobs has always been favoured with settlers having vision, capital and ambition. Their initiatives were responsible for its early prosperity and ultimate economic success. In 1847, Jacob C. Snider bought a lot by the clear, rushing Conestogo River at

Left: *Shops have replaced grain in the mill*

the site of the settlement. The river provided water for drinking and falls for power. Nearby, the German Company Tract was filling quickly with industrious German settlers and Mennonites from Pennsylvania who cleared the land and established productive farms. Snider built a sawmill, a woollen mill and a blacksmith shop to serve the growing agricultural hinterland. Soon the settlement became the service centre for farmers from this increasingly productive area.

Farmers began to call St. Jacobs "Jakobstettel," which means Jacob's village, in honour of its founder, but in 1852 it was officially named St. Jacobs. The village progressed quickly as hotels, general stores and blacksmith shops were constructed. It acquired the first creamery in the province and provided tanners, blacksmiths and coopers for its customers. Slow and steady growth ensued for a number of years.

INITIATIVE AND EARLY PROSPERITY

Elias Weber Bingeman (E.W.B.) Snider was a young miller who came to St. Jacobs in 1870. He bought the gristmill, and added new millstones and a modern water wheel. In 1875 he replaced the stones with the first steel rollers to be used in Canada, a move that gave him and the village an enormous economic advantage over all their competitors. With the steel rollers, Snider was able to process cleaner and whiter flour than other mills using traditional stone.

Later, Snider was instrumental in bringing the railway to the community, and in 1894 he electrified his mill. Soon the gaslights along the main street had been replaced by electrical fixtures. E. W. B. Snider was among the first to acquire a telephone, was elected a member of the provincial parliament, and after 1902 became a driving force behind the establishment of Ontario Hydro. His early influence on St. Jacobs stimulated its development and endures in several of its buildings.

Like many of its counterparts in Canada, St. Jacobs had attained an impressive level of economic activity and reached its peak population by 1881. It housed some 500 people and had thirty-seven businesses, totals not surpassed for over sixty years. More importantly, it offered farmers in its hinterland all of the goods and services they required. There were ten retail operations including a drugstore, millinery shop, general store and butcher. It boasted the largest roller mill in the area, a furniture factory, saddler, tailor, weaver and wagon maker. A physician, hotels and two taverns provided additional incentive to farmers visiting town to pick up their mail and conduct business. The distillery provided more than enough whiskey for the residents of the township, and despite Mennonite reservations about drinking, it persisted until Prohibition.

SLOW AND STEADY GROWTH

As long as the horse was the major mode of transportation, St. Jacobs competed successfully with its rivals. After initial rapid growth, population and business began to suffer from competition and declined to 350 and eighteen respectively by 1901. Then the number of businesses increased slowly to twenty-nine in 1941 and continued to rise to fifty in 1971. This was partially because St. Jacobs continued to function as a major shopping centre for the many Mennonites who had settled in the area. They continued to visit the village for yard goods, to have their harnesses repaired and to buy food.

A house on Albert Street

TECHNOLOGY, DECLINE AND REVIVAL

During a period of economic centralization and rapid technological change, St. Jacobs lost business to larger rivals. From the 1920s to the 1970s, Elmira to the north and Kitchener-Waterloo to the south became the premier commercial and industrial centres in the county.

By 1975, the mill and the last grocery store had closed, while Martin's Blacksmith Shop was for sale. The once proud main street was beginning to resemble that of the classic dying village, with vacant buildings and declining clientele. Despite the trade brought by Mennonites, modern trends had seriously harmed the local economy. But things were soon to improve, and the instrument of the settlement's renaissance was one Milo Shantz, a Mennonite entrepreneur.

MILO SHANTZ AND THE MERCEDES CORPORATION

Milo Shantz and his wife, Laura, had long dreamed of opening a restaurant that would specialize in traditional Waterloo County delicacies such as pork and sauerkraut, apple strudel, homemade pastries and freshly made soup. For years, people had come to see the old-order Mennonites who arrived in town by horse and buggy to shop. The Shantz family decided to exploit this curiosity by luring visitors to stay and enjoy home-cooked roast beef, freshly picked vegetables and shoo-fly (mostly sugar and maple syrup) pie. Their attempt to recreate old Waterloo County was successful. Their Stone Crock restaurant opened in 1975 and became the catalyst for unprecedented growth and development of St. Jacobs' economy.

In addition to the Stone Crock restaurant, the Shantzes and their associates created a small economic empire through the Mercedes Corporation. It eventually bought, renovated or restored almost all the commercial properties in the village. Shantz encouraged indigenous arts and crafts by gearing rents to profits rather than setting fixed rates. This nurtured artisans who might not otherwise have succeeded. Pottery, woollens, glassware, rugs, ornamental ironwork and furniture are all produced locally. Watercolours, oil painting and porcelain art by area artists are also available. Galleries, gift shops, antique shops and snack bars were established along King Street, while the Snider Mill and silos were subdivided into retail spaces and workshops.

The Stone Crock Bakery

Their twisting narrow corridors and circular rooms are a fascinating complement to the historical ambience of the silos.

TRANSFORMATION

Today St. Jacobs is renowned for its splendid local products and old-world atmosphere. A walk down King Street may leave the impression that quilting is the mainstay of the local economy. Quilted place mats, teapot covers, tablecloths and bedspreads are displayed in abundance. The Mennonite women who do the quilting follow traditional patterns such as the fan or lone star. Some may still be seen in their long black dresses (fastened by hooks and eyes) and muslin caps. Wooden toys and ice cream are available for children whose favourite stop is the train car behind the mill.

The Meetingplace is an information centre designed to educate visitors in the ways and beliefs of the old-order Mennonites. It was established by three local churches with the encouragement of Shantz. Its sophisticated audiovisual presentations contrast with the simplicity of the people it represents. A film portrays the preservation of the "plain way" and traditional family values such as lending a helping hand in times of need and "seven-days-a-week" religion. An ordinary kitchen

Visitors shopping for crafts

Mennonites on King Street

with its plain wooden table is set for dinner, its bottle of preserves and butter churn illustrating the lives of the Mennonites. To this day, old-order Mennonites farm without electricity, travel by horse and buggy and participate in communal barn raisings.

Non-Mennonite restaurants have opened for those preferring alcohol with their meals. Benjamin's offers continental cuisine and accommodation in a refurbished 1852 country inn near the river on King Street. Its attractive white-stucco dining rooms are warmed by roaring fires in the winter. Guest rooms have all the modern conveniences but feel old-fashioned. Farther along King Street, Vidalia's restaurant, which specializes in the delicate, sweet Texas Vidalia onions, delicatessens, bakeries, gift shops and cheese outlets have joined the Stone Crock restaurant in catering to tourists. A few blocks away, the Jakobstettel guest house provides a country retreat in the restored 1898 mansion once owned by E. W. B. Snider.

Photo studios, massage clinics and stores set up by spinners, weavers and leather workers have appeared and are successful. Today, the main street of St. Jacobs is busy on weekends year round, and crowded almost every day during the summer. Most shops are open seven days a week. Adding to the community's economic base is the headquarters and warehouse of the Home Hardware chain, which has existed there since 1902. It was originally the Hollinger Hardware wholesale business, but became Home Hardware in 1966. It is now one of the largest wholesale hardware firms in Canada with franchised

retail outlets across the land. The Picard Peanut processing plant and retail store were built on the edge of St. Jacobs in 1982 specifically to take advantage of the tourist trade.

TOURIST DEVELOPMENT

As St. Jacobs evolves, additional attractions are being introduced. Municipal advertising now features Ontario's Mennonite country as "an area of fertile farms worked in the old way, horse-drawn vehicles, blacksmith shops, buggy factories, wood-burning stoves, farmers' markets and a covered bridge." In 1994, a major outlet mall with over thirty businesses was established just south of the town. Nearby, St. Jacobs Market, the Flea Market, the Waterloo Market, the Stockyards and the St. Jacobs Country Inn attract increasing numbers of tourists. They offer a vast selection of fresh produce, local meats, snacks, musical groups, kites, crafts and country atmosphere in a bustling and sometimes crowded environment. Cook cheese (a smooth soft cheese made from skim milk), maple syrup, brown free-range eggs, smoked pork chops, kreiners (large smoked frankfurters), head cheese and smoked summer sausage are among the favourite Waterloo County delicacies being sold.

Statistics reflect the economic rebirth of St. Jacobs. There was an increase in the number of businesses from fifty in 1971 to 103 in 1990. Between 1975, when the Stone Crock opened and 1983, twenty new tourist-oriented businesses were established in the town. By 1985, one-third of the retail stores in St. Jacobs were devoted exclusively to tourists, while over 70 percent of all businesses derived at least half their total sales from the tourist trade.

Along with business success, St. Jacobs has achieved renewed population growth. Between 1971 and 1981 the number of residents increased from 787 to 1,189, and by 1986, the total had reached 1,525, a 94 percent increase in fifteen years. This rate of growth far exceeded that of any comparable period in the village's history. Today, with almost the same total, some 18 percent of its population is over sixty, and the settlement has attracted retirees in addition to those who just want to live in a pleasant country village.

E. W. B. Snider's 1898 mansion has been renovated and restored as the Jakobstettel Guest House

POSSIBLE PROBLEMS

St. Jacobs is an appealing, thriving tourist destination with a historic core and major peripheral attractions. The real danger is that of overdevelopment and congestion on busy weekends. Increasing economic development and growth can strain local services and create noise, dirt and traffic, eventually destroying the very attributes that encouraged economic growth in the first place. Overdevelopment has not yet become a major problem in St. Jacobs, but some undesirable effects are becoming evident. Some visitors and residents resent the parking problems, lack of privacy and crowds that accompany increasing tourism. Some are unhappy at what they see as the exploitation of the Mennonite culture for commercial

Flea market near St. Jacobs

purposes. Major changes in retailing that are not always to the advantage of local Mennonite customers have occurred. An observer said it well:

> The local farmers can no longer drive to the mill for a wagonload of feed, and they don't need furniture once a week. The stores no longer stock the dark-coloured prints, the flannelette and the full-length black hose. They do not sell flour by the hundred pounds, and peaches by the bushel. Instead, the Mennonites go to Cleason Sauder's store in Linwood, or Joe Martin's Yatton general store, or Cleason Weber's One-Stop store at Wallenstein. They are the country stores where you visit while you wait.

The major initial attraction of St. Jacobs (as well as many similar settlements) was its quaint, quiet, unspoiled small-town atmosphere and ambience. Municipal advertising presents it as "the village where time has stood still" and encourages visitors to "discover St. Jacobs, where the future is graced with the past." Some of this has been lost, even though the situation is better than in many other tourist towns. St Jacobs remains a unique and attractive destination, but one best visited on weekdays in the spring or fall.

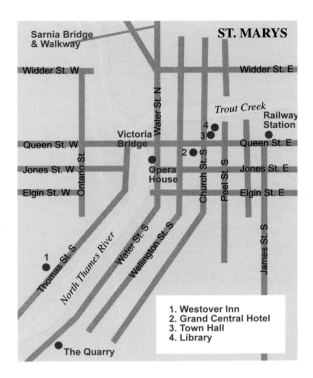

ST. MARYS

Sarnia Bridge & Walkway

Widder St. W — Widder St. E

Water St. N

Trout Creek

Railway Station

Victoria Bridge

Queen St. W — Queen St. E

Ontario St.

Jones St. W — Jones St. E

Opera House

Church St. S

Peel St. S

Elgin St. W — Elgin St. E

James St. S

Thomas St. S

North Thames River

Water St. S

Wellington St. S

1. Westover Inn
2. Grand Central Hotel
3. Town Hall
4. Library

The Quarry

ST. MARYS: A SYMPHONY IN STONE

Nestled in the valleys of the Thames River and Trout Creek, St. Marys is a symphony in stone, unique in Ontario. Towering church spires command the hills, while limestone structures reminiscent of a Scottish village line the streets and valleys. It is at the intersection of Perth County roads 123, 130, and 139, twenty-three kilometres southwest of Stratford and forty-five kilometres north of London. It is an easy two-hour drive west of Toronto. St. Marys' economic vitality, heritage architecture and river setting make it one of the most memorable towns in Ontario. The presence of a vast quantity of easily quarried limestone along the Thames contributed tremendously to its picturesque character and its early economic success. Even today, limestone is the raw material for one of its major industries.

Left: *The town hall built in 1891*

DISCOVERY AND SETTLEMENT

St. Marys was founded by Thomas Ingersoll on 337 acres that his brother James purchased from the Canada Company. In 1841, he and his party trekked inland from Beachville along the banks of the Thames through the dense and seemingly endless forest of elm, oak, maple and beech. From the foliage crowding the banks by the falls they pictured a new community.

By September 1841, Thomas Ingersoll had arranged with The Canada Company to establish sawmills and gristmills at the falls. He sent his workers ahead and later that year his family joined them to become the first permanent settlers in Little Falls. Soon, 120 people, most originally from England, Northern Ireland and Scotland, had settled. By 1843, the mills were complete and a small community had developed along the banks of the North Thames.

Lauriston Cruttenden, who had also visited the site in 1841,

61

Train station and water tower

established a general store on Queen Street in 1843. As the woods were still being cleared, he accepted potash, that valuable by-product of burning, as payment for his goods. Since farming was still in its infancy near St. Marys, the potash was hauled to London, where it was exchanged by Cruttenden for flour. Such was the bartering economy of the early days in Ontario.

In 1844, a Mr. Jones of The Canada Company visited the settlement and donated ten pounds sterling to build a school. It is reported by some that its name was promptly changed from Little Falls to St. Marys in honour of Jones' wife. Others suggest that St. Marys was actually named for Mary McDonald, wife of John McDonald who surveyed the town and Blanchard Township. He designated at least one settlement for his wife in each township that he surveyed.

EARLY ECONOMY

As the hinterland was settled, and more wheat was grown, farmers moved from subsistence to surplus agriculture. Cruttenden and a partner, Peter Murray Nicol, set up two flour mills along the river. Cruttenden also built a hotel (the National) at the corner of Water and Queen streets, established a planing mill and eventually diversified into general contracting. The natural resources of wood, water, local agriculture and stone enabled early entrepreneurs to set St. Marys

on a course towards economic prosperity. Others quickly followed, building churches, woollen mills, general stores, banks, bakeries and pharmacies.

William and James Hutton left their mark on St. Marys after 1855 by constructing six limestone buildings and what is now the Westover Hotel. The legacy of these industrious entrepreneurs and the rich building material resulted in St. Marys being nicknamed "Stonetown," a well deserved compliment to its handsome architecture. Like most Ontario towns of this era, it was the service centre for farmers within one day's return trip by horse and wagon. They came to sell their produce, shop, pick up mail and drink at the tavern.

The arrival of the Grand Trunk Railway in 1858 greatly stimulated trade, attracting not only local farmers with produce to sell, but also grain buyers from afar. As the railway's western terminus, St. Marys became the collection point for a rich and growing hinterland that produced wheat as a cash crop for export to the rest of the province. On market days, Queen and Water streets were grid-locked with horse and wagon traffic.

When the railway was extended to Sarnia in 1860, St. Marys lost its transportation monopoly, resulting in a decreased rate of growth. By the time of Confederation in 1867, agriculture, lumbering and quarrying were the basis of the local economy as the population increased slowly to just over 3,000 in 1871. New businesses were established as settlers arrived to work in the mills and shops.

ST. MARYS AT THE TURN OF THE CENTURY

In the 1900s, many stonemasons owned their own small quarries, which lined the river from the centre of town to the site of the original St. Marys Cement plant. Their efforts created the unique character that makes the settlement so attractive. For a time, immigrants were exploited to sustain building. By 1908, over a hundred Italian labourers worked in the quarries and cement plant, sometimes in appalling conditions. Shantytowns with minimal facilities housed foreign workers until the 1930s, when public concern ended their exploitation.

Once again, changing technology affected the local economy. Rural mail delivery and Prohibition after 1916 closed the pubs and reduced business in local stores. No longer did farmers have to come to town for their mail; the wonders of Eaton's catalogue were to be found in the mailbox at the end of their lane. By the 1930s, motor vehicles were widely available and roads were being improved, enabling anyone with a car or truck to bypass St. Marys for the greater variety of goods and services in Stratford or London. Growth slowed and the economy began to stagnate. Few new commercial buildings were erected. As a result, most architectural treasures escaped the ravages of the wrecker's ball, which has destroyed so many historic structures in the name of "progress." Stonetown now benefits substantially from the lack of modern development after 1930.

THE QUARRY

Physical changes also affected St. Marys' character. As time passed and the large original quarry was deepened, ground water began to infiltrate, requiring massive pumping to keep the operation viable. The area along Water Street South is now dotted with ponds and dry excavations denoting the progression of limestone extraction. The quarry became filled with water between 1930 and 1935, attracting many local swimmers and later, numerous actors from Stratford. It is now Canada's largest outdoor pool, complete with fences, rules, lifeguards and admission fees.

Lauriston Cruttenden's 1857 home on Ontario Street North

Swimming at the quarry

After the Second World War, when concrete became easier to use and less expensive than limestone, St. Marys Cement Company (now Blue Circle) replaced most small lime and quarrying operations. Just south of the swimming area are working pits from which stone is still being removed. The crushers, plant and chimneys are impressive local landmarks. Although still important to the local economy, Blue Circle now employs far fewer people than in the past. Mechanization replaced manual labour in the plant and pits.

STONETOWN TODAY

St. Marys is thriving again because of its widely diversified economy and an influx of new residents. With a population of 5,952 in 1996, the town offers much to citizen and visitor alike. It grew by 8.3 percent from 1991 to 1996, with 22 percent of its population over sixty in 1996. Its unemployment rate was then only 5.3 percent. The hospital, schools, hotels, stores, restaurants and other services provide over half the local employment. Manufacturing is shared among a number of small and medium enterprises. According to local business people, catering to tourists and providing facilities for the elderly are becoming important growth industries. Construction employed over 100 workers in 1996 as new retirement facilities and residential subdivisions continued to proliferate.

The Westover Inn

HISTORIC ATTRACTIONS

Much of St. Marys' history endures in its buildings. The salmon pink brick house of community founder Lauriston Cruttenden, which he occupied from 1857, survives at 36 Ontario Street North. Entrepreneurs William and James Hutton built their Victorian limestone mansion above the river on the western edge of town in 1867. It is now the exquisitely restored Westover Inn operated by three youthful partners whose friendliness and enthusiasm are typical of the town.

Toronto House, a limestone block constructed in 1855, which accommodates four stores, was another of the properties built for William Hutton, a prominent nineteenth-century entrepreneur. This architectural gem on Queen Street near the river acquired its mansard roof in 1884, and was the first privately owned building in town to be designated under the Ontario Heritage Act. Nearby, Victoria bridge crosses the Thames close to its junction with Trout Creek. Built in 1865 by the prominent local stonemason, Alexander McDonald, Victoria bridge was restored in 1983. It rests on strong but graceful limestone arches reflecting across the water. Upstream, the sun shimmers off the Sarnia Railway bridge beyond the falls. As a link to the outside world, this delicate, spindly structure, which was built in 1858, stimulated local prosperity.

QUEEN STREET

The Victorian Andrews Building (1884), now Anstett's Jewellery, dominates Queen Street East. Its clock tower and

mansard roof stand in stark contrast to the utilitarian glass and concrete next door. Anstett's interior has changed little from when it was built. A step inside takes visitors back 100 years, as polished walnut counters and elegant glass cases line the walls. Farther to the east, a handsome row of Victorian structures begins with the brick Hubbard Pharmacy constructed in 1883.

St. Marys' glorious Town Hall was the result of a fire that destroyed its predecessor. Rising three stories, it is one of the most impressive municipal structures in the province. This handsome building was designed by Toronto architect George Gouinlock in 1891. It was constructed of local limestone and trimmed with imported sandstone.

Andrew Carnegie's Public Library (1904) is north past the Town Hall on Church Street. Local architect J. A. Humphris designed some of its details to match the rough stone and rounded corbels of the Town Hall. Across the street is Garnett

Holy Name Roman Catholic Church

House, which was built as a hotel in 1871. Its smooth limestone exterior and mansard roof (which was the first in the town), contrast with the lavish ornamentation of the elegant Town Hall. Nearby, Timothy Eaton began his first business not far from the former Central Hotel. For anyone interested in history or architecture, Queen Street is an exciting remnant of old Ontario.

WATER STREET

One of the truly remarkable sights of Stonetown is just south of the intersection of Queen and Water streets. The former opera house is a particularly impressive structure, designed with Scottish baronial motifs by local architect Silas Weekes. It was built in 1879 by James Elliot with stone from his quarry and lime from his kiln. The scene of numerous theatrical productions, it hosted Sir John A. Macdonald on his final political campaign and echoed the voice of

Scottish soprano Jessie Mclaughlin.

During these "glory days," Water Street was as important as Queen. The Hutton Blocks (1860s) flank the Opera House. Across the street stands Damen's Restaurant, now occupying the former post office (1907), which was faced in rough local limestone. Beside it, the smooth two-storey limestone-faced block (1868) at 19 Water Street South completes one of the finest stone rows in Ontario.

HISTORIC HOMES AND CHURCHES

An impressive selection of elegant homes from the turn of the century is found on every hill. Local limestone alternates with red and soft salmon brick. Italianate, Romanesque and Victorian mansions mingle with workers' cottages and the occasional new bungalow. A stroll along Elgin, Jones, Peel and Widder streets reveals a wealth of ornate nineteenth-century homes. Farther from the core, new suburbs spread from town while a

River behind the 1897 St. Marys Opera House

recent retirement community rises on its western edge.

From a distance, steeples dominate the scene. Every major hill is crowned by a church, each attempting to exceed the others in grace and elegance. One of the most spectacular is the Holy Name Roman Catholic Church built in 1892 and designed by Toronto architects Post and Holmes.

CONTEMPORARY CHARACTER

Stonetown continues to provide the attractions and facilities characterizing a "resort, retirement, amenity" community. Its residents and shopkeepers are friendly and helpful. Its historic architecture and laid-back ambience lure new residents and visitors alike. St. Marys combines the best of small-town Ontario with modern conveniences ... and it is one of Canada's most picturesque towns to boot. Truly a hidden gem!

Public library

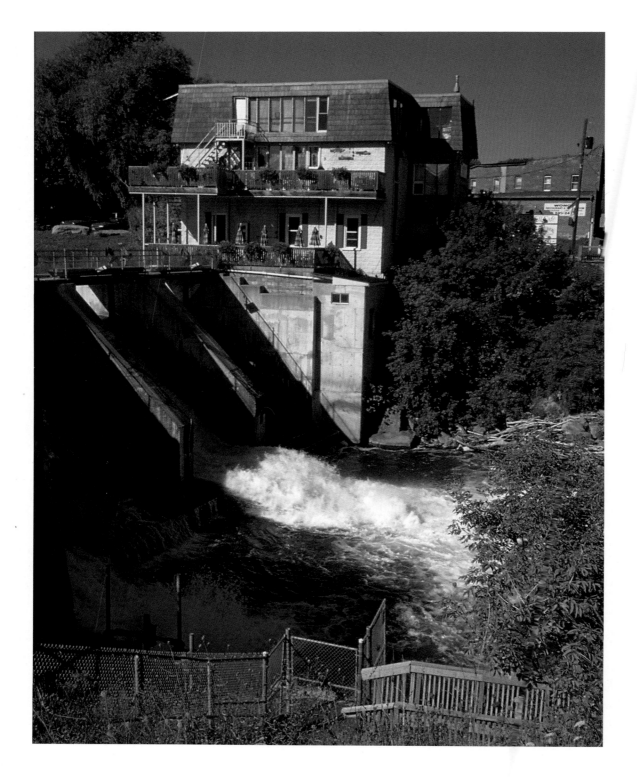

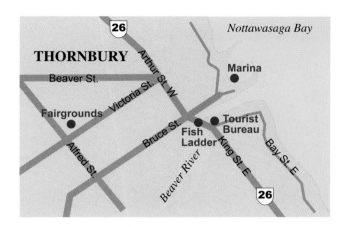

THORNBURY: FISHING AND BOATING

Thornbury is on Nottawasaga Bay, thirteen kilometres east of Meaford at the mouth of the Beaver River. The Beaver at Thornbury cuts through deep glacial deposits and then through limestone, producing some of the most spectacular scenery in the province. It is also one of the best trout and salmon streams in Ontario. Inland from the town, the drive from Thornbury to Kimberley along the rushing Beaver reveals rocky outcrops and vast rolling vistas interspersed with verdant pastures. The nearby escarpment provides outstanding ski hills, trails and locations for country residences.

EARLY HISTORY

Thornbury and surrounding Collingwood Township have a long and fascinating history. At the end of the Wisconsin Glacial Period some 12,000 years ago, fur-clad Palaeo-Indians entered the area to fish and hunt big game. Remains of mammoth and mastodon nearby indicate that these elephant-like creatures roamed the shores of Lake Algonquin, the glacial predecessor to Lake Huron. Ridges remain to mark the former Algonquin shores. After thousands of years, spruce and pine forest replaced the tundra as the ice caps receded from Ontario.

Left: *The dam and fish ladder*

Gradual warming then encouraged the establishment of hemlock and eventually mixed forest similar to that of today. Stone tools and wooden objects discovered by archaeologists indicated a hunter-gatherer economy.

By the time Samuel de Champlain visited in 1616, sedentary Wyandot people had built palisaded villages and cultivated corn in the beaver-ponded valleys east of the escarpment. These "Petun" (tobacco) people, as they were called by Champlain, shared villages with the nomadic Algonquin (Odawa) who roamed the area. They had come to trap beaver and other fur-bearing animals to trade with white settlers. Soon Jesuit priests arrived to minister to the "savages" but left in 1650 after several were martyred by raiding Iroquois, who destroyed many villages and drove the original natives away.

By the 1750s the Chippewas from the north claimed ownership of the abandoned area. They signed a treaty in that year with the King of England for 1,592,000 acres between London and Lake Simcoe for "the sum of twelve hundred pounds currency in goods at Montreal price." This set the stage for the first surveys and permanent white settlement in Collingwood Township. By the time the first permanent settlers arrived in 1818, the area had been empty of residents for many years.

Above Thornbury, the Beaver Valley opens out to Nottawasaga Bay

EUROPEAN SETTLEMENT

Charles Rankin, Ontario's deputy surveyor, had set aside 900 acres for a town at the mouth of the Beaver River but left it unsurveyed. Solomon Olmstead from Carleton County heard of recent surveys near Nottawasaga Bay and ventured into the area in the late 1840s in search of a mill site. He found a splendid location at the mouth of the Beaver River and immediately trekked to Sydenham (now Owen Sound) to register his claim. With the help of earlier settlers, he cleared a few acres for the mill and built his house by 1848. In 1852, the government surveyor, William Gibbard, came to survey the remainder of the town plot, which he named Thornbury after a borough in England.

By 1853, Olmstead was joined by his brother Rufus who helped him to build a general store and post office on the east side of the Beaver River, which was not yet bridged. When the mail arrived on Saturday, the stream was alive with canoes ferrying people from the west to collect their mail and shop at Olmstead's. By 1855, the settlement was becoming popular and the government land agent came from Durham to auction half-acre town lots for seven and eight dollars. In 1856 the railway from Barrie to Collingwood reduced Thornbury's reliance on long trips by canoe or ox cart to buy and sell goods. The railway brought the outside world to Collingwood, only fourteen miles from the fledgling community, making life much easier for those importing or exporting goods.

ECONOMIC EVOLUTION

By 1857 the settlement boasted a hundred inhabitants, a post office, general store, fanning mill, sawmill, gristmill, cooper and blacksmith. When the railway line was extended to Meaford via Thornbury the future looked promising. In 1887 Thornbury was incorporated as a town and reached its peak population and economic importance in 1891. By then, with a population of 902, it was firmly established as a port and rural service centre for those living in its hinterland. Wheat, apples, fish and lumber were produced by the fertile land and productive waters nearby. Thornbury processed the wheat and wood, stored the apples and provided services required by the settlers.

Royal Harbour Resort

Given transportation technology at the turn of the century, the vast majority of customers came from a distance easily traversed in a one-day return journey by horse, oxen or on foot. From being a complete rural service centre in 1891, it declined to a shadow of its former status by 1951, with only thirty-five businesses, compared to forty-four in the 1890s. It lost population until the Second World War, after which it began a slow recovery. In 1991 the town surpassed its 1891 population and had grown by almost 15 percent since 1981. In 1996, augmented by seniors migrating from the Golden Horseshoe and nearby townships, the population reached 1,763 — a 7.1 percent increase from 1991. During this same period, its economic functions began to evolve as well.

CONTEMPORARY THORNBURY

Today the mix of businesses in the community reflects the new realities of postindustrial society. There are no hotels, blacksmiths, mills, coopers or tanners. Instead, there are antique shops, restaurants, service stations, liquor stores, clothing stores and gift shops. Three bed and breakfasts have replaced the hotel of 1891, while hairstylists, government agencies and financial services have appeared.

While the permanent census population of Thornbury was 1,646 in 1991, there were 2,700 names on the local voters list. This is because all property owners in the town (including those owning time-share condominiums) are eligible to vote in municipal elections. The town's functional change during recent years is described in advertising literature:

> Thornbury is well-known for its specialized and unique shopping, fashion apparel and gift stores, art galleries, bookstores, fine dining and much more.

> Thornbury's marina is a major magnet for visiting vessels as well as a storage place for local boat owners.

OUTDOOR SPORTS

On the eastern side of the river is the highest and one of the more picturesque parts of the escarpment ... the Blue Mountain, which has a height of 575 metres. The Blue Mountain ski resort is one of the best-known public resorts in Ontario and has attracted tourists to the area for decades, as has the Talisman resort a few kilometres south along the Beaver Valley. The Alpine, Georgian Peaks and Osler Bluff ski clubs are private facilities that provide miles of groomed trails and downhill runs. They are also major local employers. A number of sprawling chalet communities and condominium corporations have been established in conjunction with these facilities.

Thornbury also boasts a trailer park, public beach, new arena, tourist association building and tennis courts. While the Beaver Valley and Blue Mountain offer the onlooker scenic views inland, on a sunny day much of Nottawasaga Bay's far shoreline is visible on the horizon. On "opening weekend" in April the mouth of the Beaver River is always packed with anglers. Tourism and recreation now entice more than one million visitors, who contribute over $100 million annually to the economy.

Fishing on the Beaver River

THE TOWN OF THE BLUE MOUNTAINS

In 1998, the provincial government created the Town of The Blue Mountains from Thornbury, Clarksburg and the Township of Collingwood. This act reflected provincial policy and the growing interdependence of the communities.

In the ten years previous to 1998, federal and provincial governments contributed to the modernization of Thornbury Harbour. Now recognized as one of the most popular small-craft moorings on Georgian Bay, it boasts a new administrative building, fuel dock and fish-cleaning station. Nearby, in August 1999, the former Gilchrist School Furniture building was demolished to accommodate luxury accommodations and a new subdivision was proposed on the east shore of the river. Rankin's Landing subdivision has been completed and the former Mitchell's apple-processing plant on Highway 26 is a mall and flea market.

THE APPLE INDUSTRY

Despite the demise of apple storage and processing in Thornbury, the industry is thriving in the remainder of the new municipality. As early as 1835, records indicated that the microclimate and soil were ideal for apple production. In the late 1800s, McIntosh apples were cultivated and John Mitchell grew apples, cherries, plums and raspberries. By the 1880s, packing and storing apples became big business, with facilities springing up around the area. By 1999, fruit growing was second only to tourism in the local economy with farm-gate revenues of $12 million annually. Many local workers prune, fertilize and harvest, assisted by some 600 workers from Mexico, Jamaica and the First Nations, who come to pick each fall.

Chalets and condos have displaced old orchards around Thornbury, but new dwarf plantings have increased the acreage from 3,200 in 1979 to 4,500 today. High-density methods have increased the number of trees per acre from thirty in the early 1900s to 600 trees today. There are now controlled atmosphere storage facilities for 1.1 million bushels of apples in the area.

HERITAGE ARCHITECTURE

Many of the stores along Bruce (the main) Street have the brick-faced Victorian fronts so evident in small southern Ontario towns. Nearly every store has been renovated with new facades and picture windows, but the business section retains a rustic appearance. There are three bed and breakfasts in Thornbury, with a total of thirteen rooms. Leisurely pursuits and rural ambience are reflected in the names of these establishments: the Mill Pond, Idle Inn and Golden Apple. Moreover, all three operate from Victorian houses set in tranquil surroundings.

A number of stately homes, particularly to the south and west of Thornbury's business section, grace the town's tree-lined streets. The Errinrung Nursing Home is in the house built in 1900 by lumber baron Henry Pedwell. It accommodates forty-two residents requiring extended care, as well as fifteen to twenty-six elderly people living in the second-floor retirement apartments.

Oldfield's fine dining establishment, which offers accommodations as well, is located in the town's oldest brick building, erected in 1865, and overlooks the millpond and dam.

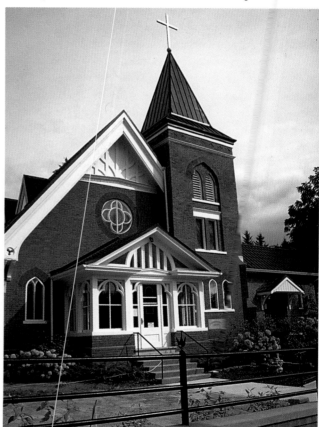

St. George's Anglican Church

Thornbury has many substantial older homes

Occupying a beautifully refurbished Victorian home in a glen across the pond is the Trillium restaurant. The Mill Cafe operates out of the old Imperial Hay building near the site where Thornbury was settled by Solomon Olmstead. These three restaurants capitalize on both the town's heritage architecture and its scenic setting. Farther from the town's core, newer structures dominate.

REAL ESTATE

As with tourism and recreation, the real estate market in Thornbury has flourished in recent years. Within two hours driving distance is a market area with a population of 5 million. A significant portion of the town's real estate market is in the buying and selling of second, or even third, homes in the area. In general, older houses in Thornbury are less expensive than their urban counterparts or new local homes.

Thornbury's three condominium developments — Applejack Corporation, Appleridge Condominiums and Rankin's Landing — are on the town's southwest edge. Housing prices in Thornbury range from $123,000 for modest townhouses to $270,000 and up for substantial older homes in the village or new waterfront locations. Overbuilding in the 1980s left many reasonably priced properties on the market.

ECONOMIC DEVELOPMENT

Given its local scenic amenities, the mix of businesses on its main street and recent residential development, Thornbury qualifies as a thriving tourist and retirement community. The number of real estate, financial and construction enterprises reflects the growing number of new chalets, cottages and condominiums catering to migrants from the Golden Horseshoe. There is no doubt that day-trippers, skiers, hikers, campers, anglers, swimmers and shoppers patronize its shops, boutiques and restaurants.

Retailing has remained the dominant economic activity in Thornbury, but the service sector has grown faster during the last two decades. A noteworthy feature of Thornbury's economic and social structure is a convergence of urban and rural lifestyles, or the transfer of an urban lifestyle to a rural setting. It is difficult to separate tourist and seasonal residents from the general population but most businesses in Thornbury rely on a mixture of patronage from locals and non-locals.

Thornbury's scenic location and friendly atmosphere appeal to locals and ex-urbanites alike. Residents refer to the Beaver Valley as "God's Country." In short, Thornbury offers small town charm and accessibility to cultural and business opportunities in Toronto.

Golden Apple Bed & Breakfast

CONCLUSION:
THE PAST AND THE FUTURE

We have met some of the new residents of Ontario's towns and villages. From the burnt-out academics refinishing furniture in Paisley, to the retirees in Thornbury, to the busy entrepreneurs of St Marys. We have discovered that there is a place for the former Torontonian among the cows and silos of the countryside. There is opportunity for the entrepreneur from Kitchener to start a business in Neustadt and there is a warm welcome in Meaford for the retired executive from London.

Along the roads between the villages we encountered workers who commute to local warehouses, enormous factory farms operated by major corporations and elegant country retreats complete with pools and riding stables. Elsewhere we found independent merchants selling crafts and antiques to tourists, owners of truck stops serving modern diesel stagecoaches and abandoned farmsteads sagging under the weight of age and neglect. The variety of people and structures has been enormous, but overall the trends are clear.

We need no longer doubt that people are returning to the country. They have flocked to commuter dormitories like Fergus and Elora, and they have swelled the populations of rejuvenated rural service centres such as Paisley and St. Marys. Each of these communities has enjoyed indigenous population growth, but in many centres, retirees from the countryside or fugitives from the city have added to the total. For those who love the land and wish for a different lifestyle, our villages and countryside have offered haven as well as opportunity.

But along with opportunity there are risks: the risk of too much development, too few services for the elderly and the possible destruction of the physical environment. The very people who rediscovered small Ontario towns now must strive to retain the assets that attracted them in the first place. Sometimes they even attempt to exclude all who follow in their footsteps and work to keep the places to themselves. The balance between growth and change, or gentle stagnation and slow evolution is difficult to achieve. Before we end our journey, let us examine this delicate balance and make some predictions for the future.

What can we say about the future of the countryside, the impact of factory farming, the demise of the rural service centre and the future of the communities that cater primarily to retirement and tourism? How have history, location, natural endowment and the activities of entrepreneurs affected our rural settlements? And what have we learned from our observations? Can we detect any trends that we would like to arrest or reinforce? Are there any opportunities for guiding the future development of our communities? Has Canada Post made a grievous error in closing so many village post offices?

It is now clear that the picture in the real world is not nearly as simple as those who have spoken of "dying villages" would have us believe. Neither is it all rosy, for there are some ghost towns and others greatly diminished from their peaks of prosperity. Some are retirement communities, others have become major resorts or tourist attractions, while others have changed little in a hundred years.

All the settlements we've investigated contain much to remind us of their history, and many display portents for the future. It is clear that many of the communities are marked by diversity, complexity and change. No simple generalizations suffice to describe them all. And yet, there are some common characteristics and processes at work. It's worth exploring the most significant of these to attempt to come up with some recommendations for common problems. These will have implications for anyone wishing to live in rural Ontario, for those who are already there and for planners, politicians and all of those who love our towns and villages.

Looking back over our travels, the communities we visited fall into a couple of different categories. Some have depended primarily on their local physical environment and its resources for their early prosperity, and today they exploit this same environment to attract tourists. Fergus and Elora belong in this category. In each of these places, entrepreneurs have exploited their historic buildings to complement local physical attractions. Others that began as rural service centres declined with the advent of motor transport, but are now important as residential settlements for retirees or those not tied to the city. Thornbury and St. Jacobs are two examples.

Others that we did not visit are isolated and have changed little in form or function over the years. Although in the minority, a few towns such as Niagara-on-the-Lake, St. Jacobs and Elora are on the verge of being spoiled by their success. In these communities, opposition to further economic development is increasing. Some others such as Neustadt and Creemore stand at the crossroads, at the threshold of popularity and prosperity, waiting for the right business to come along and invest its money.

SOME TRENDS

How can we generalize from all our impressions, from our brief visits to so many places, from the few statistics that have been available? Certainly it is not easy, but just the experience of seeing each community, of reviewing its history and of speaking to its people should point the way to a few plausible conclusions. The overwhelming first impression is that each place is unique, but this is really not so. We can distinguish between places with origins as service centres, resource communities, ports or railway towns. Today, evidence of their origins endures in every settlement, and in most, these origins have affected subsequent development.

Many former resource-based towns remain relatively far from major centres of population. They now attract development only if they are near rapid routes to major cities or if they have outstanding physical attractions. People have moved to rural service centres that are accessible to employment, or have acquired outsized functions in the form of

renovated mills or hotels. Settlements with historic forts or harbours have often been restored by new arrivals seeking profits, or by local historical associations with government help. Many have become tourist attractions. In other communities, expansive old homes, tree-lined streets and a rustic atmosphere have lured individuals who wish to retire in tranquility. Elsewhere, those places with a ski hill, conservation authority, provincial park or sandy beach have become homes to retirees or are primarily residential communities. In addition to becoming homes to migrants from other areas, some also provide amenities and attractions for day visitors.

Our observations and the data that we have collected indicate that most of the towns, villages and hamlets surveyed do indeed have some potential for modest population growth. Their quiet, shady streets, small-town ambience and access to nearby employment opportunities will continue to attract people from the city as well as from the surrounding countryside. Most have even greater possibilities for additional economic development, especially if discovered by an enterprising entrepreneur willing to take a few risks. Even though these business statistics are encouraging, we cannot extrapolate these findings to all small towns. We must not forget the former hamlets scattered across the province where all traces of earlier settlement have long since vanished. There is little to suggest that settlements that have existed only in name for many years will ever grow again.

Of necessity, most of the communities discussed were those retaining vestiges of their former functions and a few buildings that attracted residents or entrepreneurs. Our maps are covered with the names of former rural service centres that vanished entirely, and there is little prospect that they will ever reappear. On the other hand, there are numerous clusters of homes, businesses and people that are never recognized separately, simply because they are too small, or are contained within a larger statistical unit.

As we drive along country roads or visit the tiniest hamlets, we see the new residents, their homes and their businesses. To truly appreciate the significance of what is happening beyond the city, it is necessary to augment statistics with exploration and curiosity. Some of the smallest communities have the potential to grow and change, just as many that we visited have done in the last twenty years.

Statistics seldom tell the whole story, and statistics can sometimes be misleading.

SOME ANSWERS

Having considered census data and visited the actual settlements to which they refer, we are now in a position to answer some key questions. The first of these is the matter of who lives in our towns and villages today, and what do these people do? As we have seen, there is no simple answer. In the midst of the rich agricultural areas of Southern Ontario, the answer is generally straightforward. Most of those in Neustadt, Fergus and Paisley are local entrepreneurs, or employees and their families. The difference between what we find today and the situation a hundred years ago is that not everyone in business continues to depend on the surrounding rural hinterland.

Now, some operate small manufacturing or wholesale enterprises that serve large areas by truck. If they have established a restaurant, hotel or clothing outlet, they may cater to day visitors from far afield. Others are retired farmers from nearby, while some are those footloose individuals who travel a wide territory, have their own local enterprise, or drive to work in a shop or factory a few kilometres away. These are the new inhabitants of the towns and villages. Communities such as these will probably continue to increase slowly in population and business activity as long as the car and the computer continue to be widely accessible at a reasonable price.

At the other end of the spectrum we find towns like Thornbury, Meaford and Dunnville. These communities were once dependent primarily on natural resources such as lakes, forest, land or bedrock, and have found new economic stimuli from the very same sources. Their harbours, hills, rugged scenery and accessible locations have allowed them to become amenity communities where tourism and retirement are now important. They continue to function as local service centres, but increasingly provide accommodation for persons wishing to live out their days in a pleasant small-town environment. They have attracted growing numbers of tourists to swim, ski, explore or shop at their sophisticated stores. If the local architecture is extraordinary, they may also have become tourist attractions in

their own right. Depending on the enterprise of local entrepreneurs, and on the proportion of tourist-oriented stores, they may now rely more on visitors than on inhabitants or local farmers for revenue.

Isolated former fishing villages probably have little prospect for additional growth and change simply because their original *raison d'être* has either disappeared or diminished. When the mine closes in a single-industry resource town, the outlook is bleak, especially if it is situated in an area of little fertility. Remote fishing villages are no doubt scenic, but so are many that are more accessible, and they are the ones that benefit from tourism. Former lumber towns have declined, and if they lack historic architecture, easy access or outstanding scenery, they too will languish. In such places, there is little to attract the entrepreneur, the tourist or the retiree.

THE POST OFFICE

In almost every settlement in the late 1800s, the post office was combined with the general store and became a major magnet for people from miles around. Even after Prohibition killed the pubs and the motor car allowed farmers to bypass their local service centre for the city, the general store/post office endured. If one general store in a community was to survive, it was inevitably the one that everyone visited daily or weekly to collect mail. It continued to be a meeting place, a social centre, a supplier of food and hardware just because people came to it with regularity. It often contributed to the viability of surrounding businesses that would be visited on one-stop trips to main street.

We need look no further than the daily newspaper to appreciate the importance of village post office even today. Loud and vigorous protests have greeted the call for their closure, and with good reason. In many of the smallest communities, those whose economic viability is the most precarious, the demise of the post office will be a disaster. With it gone, the general stores will lose business as will all other local enterprises. Without a reason to come regularly to the main street, shoppers will go to larger places where they can find more variety and lower prices. A downward spiral will set in and we may see a repeat of the events after 1911 when rural mail delivery was introduced into Ontario. In that period, local service centres "dropped like flies," some never to recover their former status, others to disappear entirely. The same could occur again today if we are not careful. Canada Post would be well advised to consider the social and economic implications of closing village post offices, rather than worrying only about the "efficiency" of their operation. Far more is at stake than profits or losses for Canada Post in the post office closing controversy.

THE FUTURE

It is difficult to predict the future, especially if we are concerned with individual settlements, but a few generalizations are in order. First, there is the attraction of retirement in small towns with scenic amenities, accessible locations or attractive architecture. Our research, and that of many others, has shown that this is already important to the growth of many places. Statistics Canada has provided data to reinforce this view. There are now over a million Canadians older than seventy-five, and they are living longer than before. Current trends suggest that the number of Canadians over sixty-five will triple in the next forty-five years. In settlement after settlement, the percentage of the population over sixty-five has increased, to the point where many small towns can classify a third or more of their citizens as seniors. Migration data from recent studies indicate increasing flows of elderly from major cities to resort towns where they formerly had a cottage. This is already a major component of population growth in settlements as diverse as St. Marys, Thornbury, St. Jacobs and Elora. There seems to be no doubt that such trends will continue, especially as the proportion of the population over sixty increases and lifestyle considerations remain important to those choosing a retirement location.

Other contemporary studies indicate an expanding number and variety of employment opportunities in small towns or just in the "middle of nowhere." In the North, suppliers, outfitters, general stores, truck stops and craft shops proliferate in scenic locations. Farther south, feed- and seed-processing, fertilizer and pesticide dealers serve the farmer along with agribusiness consultants and wholesalers. Elsewhere, custom woodworkers, electrical and electronics fabricators or clothing and crafts manufacturers are locating

in the countryside and in some of the smallest places. They provide a new variety of opportunities for anyone wishing to live in the country or in a small town and drive to work on tranquil, scenic roads. The new inhabitants of small towns will continue to grow in number and importance until gasoline prices become prohibitive. Experience in countries with far higher energy prices than ours suggests that this will not occur for a long time to come.

Of course there are some problems lurking along with the new opportunities in our towns and villages. Some will be confronted with the decision of whether to continue to grow and therefore to install (at great cost), piped water and sewage treatment plants. Others will find that their local doctor cannot cope with an ageing population, and that the elderly have become isolated by the lack of public transport and mail delivery. Hospitals may become overextended when called on to care for those who might be better off in their own homes, but lack the necessary support services. The demand for retirement homes, nursing homes, medical care, services and transportation in our smaller settlements will create problems for some and economic opportunities for others.

Finally, we must consider the matter of our past and our future. A hundred years ago, Canada was a country of farms and forests, towns and villages. Today it is primarily an urban society, with farming employing only a fraction of its former numbers. And yet the countryside is not dead, and neither is the small town. With increasing affluence and mobility, many can indulge their desire to live on a woodlot or in a tiny village. These people have lovingly restored former schoolhouses, mills, blacksmith shops and farmhouses. Others have taken up residence in what was formerly a business on the main street of a rural service centre, or have renovated the Victorian mansion that was so long inhabited by the elderly widow. Some have built new homes within the towns and villages or in the woodlots along the concession roads. Large-scale retirement communities have been developed from scratch beside a river or lake, complete with golf courses and fishing docks. In the hills, chalets and condominiums have been constructed as first or second homes. We have rediscovered the country; we have gained a new appreciation of our past heritage; and in increasing numbers we have taken advantage of the opportunity to return to a slower, more rural way of life.

But the dangers to which we alluded above must not be overlooked. Many a quiet, rustic hamlet has been obliterated entirely by the flood of commuters from a nearby metropolis or has been overrun by industrial growth. In the opinion of some, Elora and St. Jacobs are already too crowded. They say that pressures of commercial development have almost ruined them for summer visitors and local inhabitants alike. Around the fringes of Toronto, some country roads are solidly lined with homes of rural non-farmers. In addition to creating traffic congestion and obliterating rural panoramas, these developments may compete for rich agricultural land or prevent the extraction of valuable aggregate resources. Even in the North we find strips of commercial buildings that despoil the natural environment that gave them birth.

In each of the situations described above we find conflict: quiet residential communities versus tourism and commercial growth; agriculture competing with the desire for rural residences; preservation of the natural environment against the ambition to exploit it for profit. One of the major conflicts is the desire of those who have found their ideal residential retreat to keep others out. The addition of more people will often destroy the very charm that made a village desirable in the first place, but who is to say that growth must stop soon after a place has been "discovered"?

Ironically, it is often the newcomers who wish to preserve historic architecture and the small-town atmosphere, while the "old timers" encourage population growth and economic development. Such conflicts are becoming more common and increasingly difficult to resolve. In each conflict situation we find the seeds of successful resolution along with the potential for lasting harm to the human or physical environment. Our task for the future is to strike an appropriate balance between competing aspirations for the future of our towns, villages and countryside. Such a balance will be difficult to attain, but it must occur if the country is to remain attractive to those who desire to leave the city and rediscover rural delights.

Although the popularity of small-town living is increasing, most cities also continue to grow and thrive.

But what we have seen in the towns and countryside may be a glimpse of the future. As the population ages, more and more of us will feel the desire to rediscover our roots and our heritage. And we can be sure that entrepreneurs will assist by renovating buildings, constructing subdivisions and opening new enterprises that cater to our wishes. More than a desire to leave the city, it is the aspiration to discover the countryside and to live in a tranquil and sometimes less-expensive setting that encourages so many to seek a small-town environment. The sentiment that "small is beautiful," the conservation ethic and a renewed appreciation of beauty and quality of life are at work among a growing proportion of our citizens. We will never completely recreate the settlement fabric of the 1890s, but it seems safe to say that a rural and small-town renaissance is likely to continue for the foreseeable future. The question is, will our children see the future in the same way, or will they leave the towns and villages for the city as did their ancestors before them?

If we look to the past for answers, we might conclude that our children will tire of rural and small-town life and move as quickly as possible to seek excitement and enjoyment among the bright lights of the city. On the other hand, they may be somewhat less materialistic and more idealistic than were their parents at the same age. Maybe the concern for survival, the interest in the environment, the questioning of capitalist values and aspirations will take them in a different direction. It is just possible that they will place quality of life ahead of materialistic gains, and will seek solace and contentment, or self-fulfillment in the towns, villages and wilderness of this great land. Others may emulate their predecessors of the sixties who moved to farms or rural communes to escape from threats of war, or who left the mainstream of a society that they deplored. This may occur, but trends, fads and ideals change with the times and with economic circumstances. We are reasonably certain that an increasing number of retirees and footloose workers are opting for the towns and villages in the heart of Ontario, but we will have to wait to see whether they have initiated a trend that will be followed by the young. The future of our towns and villages seems bright, but only time will tell!

APPENDIX A:
EVOLUTION OF SETTLEMENTS
AND THE COUNTRYSIDE

CHALLENGES OF EARLY SETTLEMENT

When permanent settlers finally became widely established in the late 1700s and 1800s, they faced dense forest, sometimes hostile Indians and a long cold winter. To compound the situation, surveys were often sloppy or incomplete, and the hapless pioneer had to find land from a blaze mark on a tree. In many areas, roads were nonexistent and most travellers followed the rivers and shore. Eventually, after they had discovered and occupied their allotment, settlers were required to clear and maintain half the road allowance across the front of their parcel.

Faced with dense bush, few immediate neighbours, mosquitoes, blackflies, swamp and a hostile climate, pioneers lived on the edge of starvation. For many, the situation was made worse by their urban origins and sometimes complete inexperience with farming. The nearest settlement where they could obtain supplies might be several days away, and the nearest neighbour some miles through the woods. Mere survival was the primary concern of everyone, and the first winter posed the greatest challenge.

A settler's primary task was to make a small clearing and then to use the logs to construct a rudimentary one-room shelter. Progress was slow when few tools were available and there were no neighbours to help with major chores. For many, the first winter was a time of bare subsistence, using the few supplies that they had brought from the nearest settlement.

If conditions were appropriate and the settler survived his first winter of cold and loneliness, the second year meant even more clearing, enlarging the cabin and planting wheat or other crops. Sometimes a more prosperous settler would acquire an ox, which could be used both for transportation and as a beast of burden. Even when more people had come to the area, supplies still had to be obtained from the nearest port or from a peddlar. It was usually several years until the local population could sustain a mill or general store. Until then, any surplus wheat had to be carried out, or sent in the winter by sled to the nearest port for grinding or sale.

THE FIRST VILLAGES

The majority of the first settlements were established at water power sites where sawmills processed logs into lumber to be used for more sophisticated structures. If the area prospered agriculturally, someone would soon open a gristmill near the same waterfall. Initially, the miller would grind a settler's grain in exchange for a proportion of the crop. The farmer could take his flour to bake bread and earned credits at the mill for his surplus wheat.

As time went on, a general store would be established to supply salt, sugar and other items not available locally. Eventually the economy of the settlement quickened as a blacksmith arrived to shoe horses, fabricate tools and make repairs. The inevitable distillery or brewery developed to use surplus products from the gristmill and to slake the thirst of the tavern patrons.

Settlements that became successful usually had a fertile hinterland, access to water power and one or more entrepreneurs with vision, enterprise and ambition. Luck played some part, but detailed histories of many rural service centres often hinged upon the actions of one or two key people. Even in locations that were less than ideal, an excellent entrepreneur often made the difference between success and failure. The names Adam Ferguson and the Beatty brothers are synonymous with Fergus, just as Cruttenden is with St. Marys. Some villages such as Campbellville still bear the founder's name, while in others it is long forgotten. But how could a settlement succeed without the energy and drive of a merchant, miller, tanner, cooper, wheelwright or tavern keeper?

As populations increased, religious needs were met by churches, which became among the most permanent buildings, along with the one-room schoolhouse. Then a hotel would be built to accommodate farmers or travellers making an overnight journey. Butcher shops and tanneries were established. Soon grocery stores, jewellers, dairies, drovers and even doctors or pharmacists were found in the growing communities. In some, the mills multiplied to meet local needs as did the hotels, churches and taverns. An increasing number of townspeople were accommodated in houses that soon became larger and more ornate as prosperity accompanied the growth of the rural hinterland.

The merchant who obtained the postal franchise became even more prosperous than his rivals, as almost everyone visited his premises once a week to collect mail. By the late 1800s, successful settlements boasted a main street lined with two- or three-storey business blocks, a number of substantial churches and even a factory or two down by the river. Of course, settlements that were not quite as strategically located or that lacked entrepreneurial talent often languished or fell into decline.

TRANSPORTATION AND SETTLEMENT GROWTH

If a settlement did not acquire a railway by the turn of the century, conventional wisdom suggested that it was "doomed." Consequently, many schemes were developed to lure the "iron horse" to each and every aspiring metropolis. In some cases the new railway would bring prosperity as the settlement gained access to larger markets, coal supplies for its industry and transportation for its travellers.

Contrary to expectations, many places were not affected at all, simply because the railway was of no value to the farmer bringing crops to town. He still had to trek to the mill with his horse and cart to deliver grain for processing. He still came to the local settlement to shop, collect his mail, visit and drink at least once a week. Sometimes stagnation set in when a nearby town, as a result of its long-distance import/export connections, acquired new industry and forged ahead of less-fortunate rivals. But far fewer places actually died of "railroad deprivation" than conventional wisdom would have us believe.

Another innovation in transport technology, the motor vehicle, did deal a death blow to many, but not until much later.

Railways were the most modern mode of transport until the early part of the twentieth century, when the car and truck began to appear in even remote locations. Unlike the railway, motor vehicles had a devastating effect on many towns and villages. Not only did they make it possible for anyone to bypass the local service centre for a larger place a few kilometres beyond, but they also fostered rural mail delivery and catalogue shopping. Why patronize the local general store when the wonders of Eaton's and Simpsons were only a postage stamp away? Now that mail was delivered to the end of the lane, there was less need to visit the local village and the great decline began. It is this decline that many still remember and cite as the reason for their "dying villages."

To compound matters, Prohibition, along with Victorian attitudes, church groups and the Women's Christian Temperance Union, conspired to close the pubs that had remained a stellar attraction in rural settlements. No more joining the boys for a whiskey or beer after the long day of planting or harvesting. No longer was it legal to quaff the spirits in order to raise one's spirits in the company of friends. Hotels, pubs, taverns and with them hamlets and villages, dropped like flies. In some locations, derelict and rotting buildings remain to remind us of this carnage. Elsewhere, the old hotel has been given a new life through restoration and has become a key factor in settlement rejuvenation. Many hotels were simply converted to residences or were torn down. The abandoned hotel remains a symbol of the dying village.

Between 1911 and the 1960s, changes in technology, attitudes and the economy reduced businesses and populations in many of Canada's smallest communities. Some villages are now nothing more than a stand of lilac bushes, overgrown ruins at the edge of a plowed field or names on a map. Others retain the ruins of a church or school, a house or two, a ramshackle mill or a vacant hotel.

REVOLUTIONS IN FARMING

Towns, villages and hamlets aren't the only things that have changed during the last hundred years. Farming too has been revolutionized with the advent of mechanization, large-scale operations and agribusiness. Such changes have had an impact on the settlements, sometimes positive, but often negative.

We all agree that farms are generally bigger now and that agribusiness has replaced the family farm. This ultimately means fewer people for the local store, church, school and social club. It means less local community spirit and less opportunity for the young as fewer people and more machines are required to operate a diminishing number of larger farms. Tenants and absentee corporate landlords have often replaced the closely knit farm family of the past.

The effect of these changes may be seen in the land and in the villages. Empty storefronts dot the main streets. The windows of upper stories, no longer used as residences, stare blankly out at the old mill, which has fallen into disrepair, or at the railway station, which is closed and boarded up. Abandoned farmhouses stand gaunt against the sky, close by the skeletons that have been stripped for barn board by scavengers from the city. Woodlots have disappeared, streams have been straightened, concreted and sanitized (only to be polluted by runoff from chemical fertilizers).

Wooden cedar-rail fences have gone, and four or five former farms have been combined to produce corn or soybeans efficiently. The large, high, gable- or gambrel-roofed Central Ontario barn has been replaced by long low metal buildings in which hapless cattle, pigs or poultry are fed the fruits of the land. Enormous blue or silver silos pierce the sky like giant fertility symbols to hold the feed derived mechanically from the earth. Between every eight or ten lots we find the ruined foundation of a church or school, or the clump of trees that shaded former congregations.

Here and there new bungalows eat away at the edges of the farms, or snuggle in the few remaining woods along the rear survey lines. No more the even, hundred-acre patchwork of mixed farming, houses, barns, silver streams and picturesque hedgerows along the wooden fences. Modern technology has taken over, and it shows.

Ironically, this scenario is most frequently found in areas settled relatively recently. Our ancestors often made errors in their assessment of farmland and originally took up stony or hilly sites that appeared fertile because they were densely forested. When we search for the old rural landscape almost as it was, we need only drive to parts of Eastern Ontario, Southern Wellington County or the uplands of Central Ontario. Here the old log barns share space with their two-bay successors or the more recent Central Ontario barns. Here lie the remnants of our earliest villages, but even in these remote or infertile areas, change is coming as the wave of migrants from the cities begins to roll across the land.

THE LAND BETWEEN THE VILLAGES

The land between the villages has changed tremendously during the last hundred years. In many ways, the nucleated settlements have been less susceptible to metamorphosis than their rural hinterlands, simply because of the inertia of fixed capital. When roads, hotels, houses, mills and churches are built, they become permanent features of the landscape, far less subject to alteration or replacement than a farmstead or field pattern.

In the evolution of the countryside, fence lines, barns, houses and cleared land have undergone a continuous evolution, as farming practices have varied over time. First the log lean-to, surrounded by dense bush; later the log house in the centre of several stump-filled acres; then the frame house and two-bay barn; finally a brick Victorian house and Central Ontario barn commanding over sixty acres of cleared land and forty or more of bush. In contrast, the original mill or its early replacement may remain in the village, while the main street has changed little since its origins. Houses and hotels built over a hundred years ago may have a different function now, but they are easily recognized by their form. But before we examine the changing functions of villages and hamlets in detail, we must describe the events that occurred in the countryside around them.

The economy of the hinterland is invariably reflected in its service centres, and in agricultural areas, this economy has been imprinted on the land. Evolving farming practices responded to economic conditions in the rest of the country, just as villages responded to the needs of their hinterlands. The natural environment, so briefly described in chapter one, set the limits and provided the potential for agriculture in Ontario. In each area it gave rise to unique patterns of land use and settlements. We will now turn our attention to these changing mosaics of land use.

For the first few years, there was little visual difference between the initial attempts at agriculture anywhere in

Ontario. Almost everywhere the pioneer was faced with impenetrable bush, a difficult climate and poor transportation. Upon arriving in the new land he would normally stop at the local administrative centre to claim his property and pick up a few supplies.

Only in the extreme southwest of Ontario and in parts of the Ottawa Valley, which were settled originally by the French, can we find linear settlement patterns similar to Quebec's seigneurial rangs. The vestiges of such early French surveys still remain around Windsor, Amherstburg and La Salle at one end of the province, and near Hawkesbury at the other. Otherwise, Ontario's survey system and the resultant settlement pattern are very different from that found in Quebec. Most early villages in Ontario focus on dam sites or crossroads.

The landscape and character of Ontario are also distinctive. Almost every aspect of its history discussed in this book remains somewhere on the land today, providing a unique opportunity to explore our agricultural heritage and discover first hand how it is related to our village legacy. An appreciation of farming practices, farm buildings and the land may turn a casual journey out of the city into an exciting adventure.

Most of Ontario was surveyed before the settlers were granted their land. In typically bureaucratic fashion, most of the province was divided into a neat geometric pattern that had little do with the topography. The first surveys began along the St. Lawrence and followed the lakes. Baselines were laid out roughly parallel to the lake or river, and townships were surveyed inland from the baseline. Depending on the survey method used, lots for individual settlers were one or two hundred acres, forcing a dispersed settlement pattern. Farm lots were laid out along concession roads that generally trended east-west, and side roads were blazed between every fifth or sixth lot in a north-south direction.

Despite the fact that a number of different survey methods were used, and that baselines deviated from an east-west orientation as surveys proceeded inland, the net result was a geometric landscape of roads intersecting at right angles, dispersed farmsteads of more or less uniform size and a need for service centres to provide a focal point for trade and commerce. In anticipation of this need, town plots were laid out in most original townships, but more often than not, failed to become the local settlement site. Soon the practice of surveying town-

sites in every township was abandoned, and old maps often provide the only evidence of their intended existence.

The distinctive grid of Ontario concession roads and sideroads was a direct result of the survey system, just as the evenly spaced pattern of towns and villages in the late 1800s was also its legacy. By then it seemed that every other crossroads had a hotel, tavern, general store or blacksmith shop. In many areas, human error compounded by swamps, rain, heat, cold, black flies and mosquitoes left its mark in sharp road angles where two surveyors coming from different directions didn't quite meet.

Elsewhere, roads charge recklessly up the steep sides of hills or escarpments, or plunge into a lake because the line of survey crossed at that location. Where counties or townships meet, strange angles and peculiar road patterns break the consistent geometric grid. Despite these aberrations, Ontario's original survey left a lasting impression on the landscape, producing a checkerboard of farms of roughly equal size, with a house and barn near the front and a strip of bush along the back of lots that were never cleared.

THE FIRST SETTLERS

The settlement of Southern Ontario began in earnest after 1800 when Americans came from the south to take advantage of Crown land being offered for sixpence an acre plus survey costs and an oath of allegiance. The first arrivals came in from the south or east and generally followed the St. Lawrence and the Great Lakes. As time went on, both the surveys and the settlers penetrated the land to the north and west. A key to interpreting the settlement history and architecture of Ontario is to remember that the earliest settlements and buildings were found near the lakes, and that the progression was generally from the east to the north and west. House types built in Kingston in the 1850s would not be seen in the Bruce Peninsula until the 1880s. The same is true of barn types and agricultural practices.

The first settlers came to an administrative centre such as Newark (now Niagara-on-the-Lake), York or Guelph and determined the location of their land. Then began the arduous journey along lake and river and then overland to their plot. In the early years there were few roads, and those that existed were nothing more than rough trails between the trees. Settlers preferred the relatively open, oak parklands along Lake Erie and avoided swamps or moraine. Since clearing was the major task confronting the settler, the lightly forested oak-hickory woods were preferred to the wetter sites supporting beech, maple and basswood.

At first the evaluation of land was somewhat haphazard, because settlers had little experience with North American vegetation. Often they would choose a heavily forested area, only later to discover that the trees had covered thin acidic soil that would not sustain agriculture. But as time went on, settlers' guides provided more useful information on site selection, and the settlers made more appropriate choices. Those from the United States had experienced similar conditions before and generally fared considerably better than those from the British Isles.

Aside from the fertility of the soil and the ease of clearing, the major factor in site selection was access to a settlement with a mill, or at least proximity to a road. Not only was loneliness a major hazard of the early forest, but settlers who wished to advance beyond the subsistence level had to have a market for their produce. For many years the main commercial crop was wheat, which had to be transported to mill and market.

EARLY FARMING

In his first year, a settler would clear a small area by girdling the trees and then planting a few vegetables and possibly some wheat in the clearing. His animals, which might be a pig or two and an ox, were allowed to forage for themselves in the woods. Amid the gloom of enormous trees and far from any neighbours, the pioneer would spend most of his waking hours girdling trees and clearing underbrush. His first home was a one- or two-room cabin built of logs cut from his clearing. Later, when he had cleared more land and possibly some of the road allowance across his property, a second home, generally of squared timbers and in simple Georgian style was built. This structure might have one and a half stories, a fireplace and an earth cellar beneath. In Eastern or Northern Ontario, on the Bruce Peninsula and in parts of Southern Ontario that were settled early and abandoned, remnants of this era remain in both houses and barns.

The barn was the chief processing point for the agricul-

tural economy, and soon came to dominate the rural landscape. The first permanent barn was called a two-bay barn, and facilitated wheat monoculture. This barn stood about twenty by ten metres and had double doors on both long sides. On one side of the doors a bin for wheat was found, and on the other, a storage area and possibly a small stable.

The wheat was threshed by opening the doors, flailing it and allowing the wind to blow the chaff away. In this system of agriculture, one field was planted in vegetables for the family, one was sewn down to wheat and another was allowed to lie fallow. The scene was untidy, with logs lying as fences at the side of cleared fields, stumps everywhere, cattle, sheep and hogs wandering in the forest, and the ever present edge of the woods awaiting clearance looming over the scene.

The successful farmer made good use of all the products of his land. Logs could be sold, ashes could become potash and bark could be used for tanning. If he had cleared enough land, surplus wheat became available in the second year, which was required by new settlers who needed food for their first year. This very rapid emergence of commercial agriculture was contingent upon one's ability to transport grain to a location where it could be milled and traded. Across Ontario, at almost every viable water power site, mills were established to saw lumber and grind the grain. These embryo rural service centres were established to meet the needs created by a growing commercial-agricultural economy.

When more settlers arrived and the economy quickened, farmers moved into the next phase of agricultural production. Better roads and growing populations stimulated the demand for meat and dairy products, and farm buildings were adapted or replaced to accommodate these needs. Sometimes the old two-bay barn was raised onto a foundation to create a stable beneath and provide space for hay storage above. By the 1850s, in prosperous areas, the two-bay barn was often replaced by the much larger Central Ontario barn with a gable roof. This building had a large loft above for hay storage, a drive floor and grain bins on the main level for storing equipment, and crops and stables beneath. A version called the bank barn was built into the side of a hill to allow direct access to either the stable or drive floor. Later versions were built with lumber trusses rather than timber bents, and are distinguished by their gambrel roof. They provided considerably more storage in the loft and became common in the 1880s.

In Waterloo County and in parts of Bruce and Grey, the German settlers from Pennsylvania built a substantial barn with an overhang or forebay over the stable, called the Pennsylvania barn. It had Dutch doors at the end of each row of stalls, which were arranged at right angles to the long side of the barn. Unlike the two-bay barn, the Pennsylvania barn was large and flexible and generally was not replaced. In prosperous Mennonite areas of Waterloo County, the Pennsylvania barn is now surrounded by silos and cattle sheds, and is sometimes unrecognizable.

In areas where dairy farming became commonplace, the Wisconsin barn, which was promoted for scientific agriculture by the Ontario Agricultural College, replaced the two-bay barn by the turn of the century. It is a large lumber-frame barn with many windows and a gambrel roof lined with ventilators. It has milking parlours on the main floor and large storage areas above. Where agribusiness has become important, the Wisconsin barn is often surrounded by large blue or silver silos.

When travelling in rural Ontario, one finds the most modern barns in prosperous areas that have undergone rapid change. Two-bay barns and early predecessors are often discovered in economically marginal areas, or in those that were settled early and subsequently bypassed because the settlers had misjudged their fertility. Everywhere, the barn faithfully mirrors the past and present agricultural economy of the area. Dairying is important where Wisconsin barns predominate. Beef cattle is associated with the Pennsylvania barn, which is surrounded by silos and long low metal sheds. Specialty crops such as apples are produced where the small, distinctive Erie Shore barn with its overhanging roof is found. Of course, agribusiness has changed the scene in some areas as two-storey poultry barns stretch along the ground or where hogs are found in similar structures surrounded by circular metal feed storage containers. Nevertheless, in most areas, the early legacy may be found and used to glimpse the past.

Farmhouses evolved along with the barns. After the first rude shelter, a second Georgian-style edifice was built of logs, and then a more ornate Victorian home of brick or batten board often became the final replacement. These now stand as examples of Ontario vernacular architecture, with their ornate fretwork and steep roof lines. In Bruce County they are built of fieldstone; elsewhere of red or yellow brick. Where limestone was abundant, many are of that material. Numerous regional variations exist, with differences in local styles or materials. Some believe that the farmhouse was a major symbol of success and prosperity in nineteenth-century Ontario. More recent farmhouses are often little different from the suburban bungalow in the city or town.

THE RISE OF AGRIBUSINESS

The family farm has been the mainstay of Ontario's rural economy for a hundred years, but is being threatened or replaced by agriculture that relies on corporate methods and large-scale production. Instead of planting a vegetable garden, growing some wheat to sell and hay and corn to feed to animals and producing some cream for profit, the new farmer plants one crop exclusively in an environment that some feel is more akin to industry than to agriculture. This specialization is made possible by mechanization and land holdings of 500 or more acres. Now huge machines chemically fertilize the land and apply weed killer, while others plow vast swaths and plant the seed over hundreds of acres. Harvesting is accomplished with self-propelled combines, corn harvesters or soybean pickers. The enormous investment in equipment means that extensive acreages must be cultivated to make the business profitable, and that fences must disappear to accommodate the machinery. It also means that one person can accomplish the work that occupied a whole farm family ten years ago.

As a result of the new farming technology, a way of life and a set of familiar buildings have been replaced. Now hundreds of acres may be devoted solely to the production of corn, which is stored and fed to cattle that never leave their feedlot. Elsewhere, acres of soybeans, rapeseed (canola) or sunflowers have replaced the traditional mixture of wheat, oats and hay. Along with these changes has come the demise of the family farm. Corporations have bought several one-hundred-acre operations, or successful farmers have taken over their neighbours' land to achieve economy of scale. The result has been a decline in rural farm populations and the disappearance or obliteration of traditional farm buildings.

In the richest agricultural areas in Southern Ontario, farmhouses stand empty and abandoned, while barns are stripped of boards for suburban recreation rooms. We find more and more modern bungalows or split-level houses, and an increasing number of long, low metal buildings where barns once stood. Gleaming, round, metal, feed-storage containers surround the new factory farm, and enormous seed and feed-cleaning plants dot the countryside. And now the fences are gone, creating a landscape in Ontario that is sometimes more reminiscent of the Prairies than of its own agricultural heritage. The change has been profound and is clearly visible on the land.

THE RURAL NON-FARMERS

During the last ten years, the number of farmers has dropped dramatically as new methods and urban pressures have taken their toll. What is the detailed pattern of the move back to small towns and the countryside? Where have the newcomers come from and why did they reverse what seemed to be the inexorable trend towards the cities? What physical, social and economic impact have they had upon the countryside and how are they viewed by their new rural neighbours?

A large number of these modern-day immigrants have moved into rural towns and villages across Ontario, but many have also located in the open countryside. Now that the population of non-farmers in rural areas is almost five times that of farmers, the look of the land has been altered to reflect that fact. Within thirty kilometres of our big cities, especially where there is rolling or scenic land, the wealthy have built their estates. Here we find majestic mansions on ten or twenty acres, complete with riding stables, swimming pools, tennis courts and three-car garages. The owners are often affluent executives from the city who crave the solitude of the country and can afford both the time and the money to commute daily to their workplace.

On land not quite so favourably endowed sometimes at the edge of an existing village or hamlet, we find subdivisions of two-storey houses, bungalows and split-level homes on lots up to several acres. Again, the inhabitants are often commuters who seek the quality of life and relaxed living that the country is supposed to bring. Neat, manicured lawns with sweeping driveways and landscaped streets sometimes provide a jarring contrast to the hog or beef feedlot only a few hundred yards away. At times the conflict is more than visual, as former city dwellers object to the noise and smells of their rural neighbours.

Contrary to conventional wisdom, commuters do not constitute the majority of rural non-farm dwellers. The phenomenon of country living has spread well beyond the one-hour commuting time that some will spend to drive to the city. Non-farm people are now found in the countryside in relatively isolated areas far from the cities. Here they live, work and play, seldom having contact with metropolitan areas. The countryside reflects this new lifestyle: a former schoolhouse converted to a residence complete with fireplace and satellite dish; a cottage that has been insulated and equipped with year-round facilities; a hobby farm beside an artificial lake stocked with trout; a rustic log cabin fully insulated and boasting solar heating. All these are the physical manifestations of a major shift away from urban living.

Some non-farmers are less glamorous than those living in the homes described above. We still find the part-time farmer who holds a job at the local feed mill and keeps a few pigs or chickens to supplement his income. Another may drive a truck for the county and lease a hundred acres to run some sheep. Increasingly we find retirement villages tucked into the woods at the edge of productive farmland. These are often composed of prefabricated or mobile homes and boast a resident nurse, recreation hall and golf course. The seniors have sold their houses in the town or city to retire beside a lake or woods, where they can enjoy low taxes and quiet surroundings. Sometimes the elderly have converted an abandoned farmhouse, just as the yuppies have taken over some of the best examples of stone and brick farmhouses made redundant by factory farming.

In many of our best agricultural areas, a new bungalow may be found along the concession road a few hundred yards from the farmstead. Here a son or daughter has built on ten acres severed from his or her father's land, or the elderly parents have retired and leased farm and house to a younger person. Along the side roads, especially if they lead towards an urban area, we find everything from cottagelike chalets to substantial houses nestled into the woodlots that have been left along the "back forty." Many have retained the woodland atmosphere (complete with mosquitoes and black flies) and attempted to integrate their houses into the rustic settings. Unfortunately, these and the other non-farm residents of rural areas often demand improved roads, schools and local services, all of which increase local taxes and sometimes lead to conflicts within farm communities.

The overall impact of these non-farm inhabitants upon our rural areas varies widely. North of Toronto it is enormous, as one residential estate follows another and the rural roads are now mostly paved. Driving through these areas is reminiscent of a trip through Connecticut or Westchester County. Farther afield, along the escarpment or moraines, summer residences or converted chalets often outnumber farmhouses, many of which were abandoned when the poverty of the soil became apparent. In the best agricultural areas, where zoning and severance regulations are strict, the major impact is in the woodlots or on farms where a second house was built before the concern for preserving agricultural land arose.

Non-farm residential development is encouraged in or adjacent to hamlets or villages where urban services can be provided. Along the Bruce Peninsula, beside the lake or near ski slopes, the process continues as cottages are converted to year-round use and new homes are built for winter and summer recreation or retirement.

THE NEW RURAL LANDSCAPE

A major transformation has overtaken the countryside of Ontario. We may still find the traditional farmstead with its Central Ontario barn, wooden silo, abandoned windmill, brick Victorian farmhouse, lumber driving shed and hundred acres of mixed grain, pasture and bush. In many areas, the cedar rail fences lined with raspberry bushes and wild apple trees continue to surround farms that have existed unchanged for a hundred years. But these are becoming less common as the new replaces the old, the business of farming replaces the family farm and the self-propelled harvester replaces the tractor and combine. This is especially true within a hundred kilometres of the major cities, where both commuters and the new rural dwellers vie with agribusiness for our rural land.

Farther afield, in rugged or scenic areas, and near the lakes, farmers compete with those desiring a rural amenity area as their place of residence. Remnants of the old ways remain, especially on patches of level and fertile soil that are not appealing to the new non-farmers. Happily enough, the competition with agriculture is less severe in scenic areas

simply because the very ruggedness that once discouraged agriculture now attracts those desiring a rustic lifestyle.

If present trends continue, we will observe fewer and fewer, but considerably larger farms in the future. Our rural countryside will become even more like that of New England, where wealthy exurbanites wield more economic power and political influence than the former locals. More of our old mills and blacksmith shops in the country will become antique shops or artists' studios, and additional surplus farmhouses will accommodate those who need only a computer terminal and a modem to carry out their business. Meanwhile, the population will age, as the young leave for the city and their parents grow older and are joined by others from city or town who crave the quiet of the country.

For some this scenario presents economic opportunity. Owners of marginal farmland may find their property in demand for cottages, ski chalets or retirement residences. For others it presents a challenge, as they see a traditional way of life disappearing from rural Ontario and agriculture being spoiled by newcomers' demands for silence, better roads and odourless air. Politicians and planners are confronted with conflicting demands and the need to reconcile different agendas for the countryside. Some have suggested that the pressure will decrease when the price of petroleum rises even more, but this has not yet been the case in North America. Even in Europe, where fuel is much more expensive, the trend to move to the country has not diminished.

This then is the historical background and context of our journey into the villages and hamlets of Ontario. The size and function of these settlements may vary from one region to another, but their initial functions were similar and their evolution is often parallel. The symbiotic relationship between forest and lumber town, minerals and mining town, agriculture and market town has endured, and to a large extent, the nucleated settlements continue to reflect their hinterlands in form and function. Like the countryside however, they too have changed through time, sometimes in response to stimuli from the country, sometimes as a result of the return of population to the village. Intimate settings, heritage architecture, clean air, and inexpensive housing have attracted people to towns and villages, just as they were once attracted to the countryside.

APPENDIX B:
STATISTICAL PROFILES OF THE TOWNS

Because of random rounding, percentages may not total 100%. Population and average family (husband and wife) income figures are for 1996. Recent local government reform has included a number of the following municipalities in reorganized units. As noted below, their occupational and income data are for the whole municipality, which contains rural areas and other municipalities. Web site addresses refer to the most useful links available. The Ontario Government Municipal Web site (http://199.202.235.157/ylg/ontario.html) contains links to all municipalities with web sites, and information on local government reform (old and new names, areas, et cetera).

CREEMORE
1996 Population: 1285
Clearwater Township Web site is not yet operating
Location:
A kilometre west of Airport Road; 1.5 hours north of Toronto; 30 kilometres south of Collingwood and Georgian Bay
Nursing and Retirement Homes:
Creedan Valley Nursing Home, operated by Leisure World
Other Services:
Five churches; junior and senior primary public schools; public library affiliated with Simcoe Public Library; Teddy Bear's Picnic Daycare
Medical Facilities:
Creemore and District Health Centre: chiropractic, dental, medical, x-ray
Recreational Facilities:
Arena; ball park; tennis courts
Recreation, Sports, Other Groups and Facilities:
Baseball club; Beavers and Cubs; curling club; hockey clubs; horticultural society; lawn bowling club; Lion's Club; Masonic Lodge; Orange Lodge; Purple Valley Heritage Society; skating club; snowmobile club; tennis club; veteran's club
Other Attractions:
Hiking and snowmobile trails; excellent fishing

Real Estate:
Some small homes in the village available from $130,000. Many estates on large lots, homes in new peripheral subdivisions and nearby farms from $180,000 to over $500,000. Lots available in the countryside from $17,000.

Employment (Clearwater Municipality):

Agriculture and Related	9%
Fishing	0%
Logging	0.2%
Mining	0.4%
Manufacturing	19%
Construction	9%
Transportation and Storage	4%
Communication and Utilities	2%
Wholesale	5%
Retail	14%
Finance/Insurance	2%
Real Estate	2%
Business Service	5%
Government Service	5%
Educational Service	5%
Health and Social Service	9%
Accommodation/Hospitality	7%
Other Services	6%

Average Income of Husband and Wife Family in 1996:
$51,607 (Clearwater Municipality)

DUNNVILLE
Web site:
http://www.ontariotowns.on.ca/dunnville.shtml
1996 Population: 5,043
Location:
At the mouth of the Grand River on the north shore of Lake Erie on Highway 3; 1.5 hours west of Toronto
Nursing and Retirement Homes:
Grandview Lodge Nursing Home; Lalor Retirement Home

Other Services:

Community Information Centre; daycare centres; fourteen churches; Heron Landing "Adult Lifestyle Community"; high school; junior and senior primary public schools; public library; seniors' support services and three seniors' clubs

Medical Facilities:

Chiropractic; dental; medical; massage; naturopathic practitioners; Haldimand War Memorial Hospital is full service and twinned with Hagersville Hospital

Recreational Facilities:

Arena; ball park; bird watching; camping (four local facilities); Byng Island Conservation Area; boat rentals; Grand River cruises; Lion's Park Swimming Pool; marina; outfitters; fishing guides; tennis courts

Recreation, Sports, Other Groups and Facilties:

Baseball club; Big Sisters; bowling club; Cubs and Scouts; curling club; Four H Club; golf and country club; Girl Guides; hockey clubs; horticultural society; Junior Farmers; Kinsmen; Lion's Club; Lioness; Masonic Lodge; Orange Lodge; Royal Canadian Legion; Royal Canadian Air Force Reunion; sailing club; skating club; soccer club; tennis club

Other Attractions:

Accessible to excellent fishing, hiking, boating, swimming, camping, bird watching along the river

Real Estate:

A number of homes and condominiums in the town are available from $79,000. Estates on large lots, homes in new peripheral subdivisions and nearby farms from $100,000 to well over $400,000. Many properties are listed in all price ranges.

Employment:

Agriculture and Related	12%
Fishing	0%
Logging	0%
Mining and Quarrying	1%
Manufacturing	21%
Construction	6%
Transportation and Storage	5%
Communication and Utilities	3%
Wholesale	3%
Retail	13%
Finance/Insurance	2%

Real Estate	1%
Business Service	3%
Government Service	3%
Educational Service	6%
Health and Social Service	10%
Accommodation/Hospitality	6%
Other Services	7%

Average Income of Husband and Wife Family in 1996: $46,034

ELORA

1996 Population: 3,346

Web site:

http://www.mytown.ca/ontario/towns/elora/index.htm

Nursing/Retirement Homes:

Wide availability throughout Guelph and Wellington County; Community Care Access Centre

Other Services:

Junior and Senior Primary Public Schools

Public Library

Six churches

Medical Facilities:

Access to hospitals in Fergus and Guelph; Chiropractic; Dental; Massage

Recreational Facilities:

Arena

Ball Park

Elora-Cataract Trailway (hiking, skiing, snowmobiling)

Elora Gorge Trail

Gorge Park

Grand River Conservation Authority: camping, swimming, river rafting on tubes

House tours

Squash courts

Tennis Courts

Wellington County Museum and Archives

Recreation, Sports, Other Groups and Associations:

Baseball Club

Bowling Club

Car Club (Elora Village Cruisers)

Community Theatre

Cubs and Scouts

Curling Club
Elora Festival
Fishing on the Grand River
Four H Club
Girl Guides
Golf nearby
Hockey Clubs
Horticultural Society
Junior Farmers
Karate Club
Kinsmen
Lion's Club
Masonic Lodge
Orange Lodge
Royal Canadian Legion
Skating Club
Soccer Club

Other Attractions:
A wide variety of shopping for daily needs as well as antique shops; hand-made jewelry; clothing; art and print galleries; hotel, motel, B & Bs; restaurants from gourmet to take-out; craft supplies; historic architecture

Real Estate:
A wide variety from heritage stone houses to modern condominiums on the river, to cottages to standard new subdivisions to nearby estate and farm homes. Prices range from $100,000 for condominiums and nearby cottages, to $150,000 for a modest house in the village to over $800,000 for heritage farms. Lots start at $62,000 and new houses in subdivisions are from $175,000 up.

Employment:

Agriculture and Related	3%
Fishing	0%
Logging	1%
Mining and Quarrying	1%
Manufacturing	20%
Construction	7%
Transportation and Storage	4%
Communication and Utilities	1%
Wholesale	4%
Retail	12%
Finance/Insurance	5%
Real Estate	1%
Business Service	4%
Government Service	2%
Educational Service	8%
Health and Social Service	10%
Accommodation/Hospitality	11%
Other Services	8%

Average Income of Husband and Wife Family 1996:
$61,174

FERGUS

1996 Population: 8,884
Web site: http://www.gri.ca/fergus/ferguslinks.html
Nursary/Retirement Homes:
Wide availability throughout Guelph and Wellington County
Community Care Access Centre
Other Services:
High School
Junior and Senior Primary Public Schools
Montessori School
Public Library
Seven Churches
Medical Facilities:
Groves Memorial Hospital; Chiropractic; Dental; Massage
Recreational Facilities:
Arena
Ball Park
Swimming Pool
Elora-Cataract Trailway (hiking, skiing, snowmobiling)
Grand River Conservation Authority: camping, swimming, river rafting on tubes
House tours
Templin Gardens
Tennis Courts
Wellington County Museum and Archives
Recreation, Sports, Other Groups and Associations:
Baseball Club
Big Sisters
Bowling Club
Curling Club
Classic Car Show
Community Theatre

Cubs and Scouts
Curling Club
Four H Club
Fishing on the Grand River
Golf
Girl Guides
Highland Games
Hockey Clubs
Horticultural Society
Junior Farmers
Karate Club
Kinsmen
Lion's Club
Market
Masonic Lodge
Orange Lodge
Royal Canadian Legion
Skating Club
Soccer Club
Theatre on the Grand
Truck Show

Other Attractions:

A wide variety of shopping for daily needs as well as antique shops; hand-made jewelry; clothing; art and print galleries; motels, B & Bs; restaurants from gourmet to take-out; craft supplies

Real Estate:

A wide variety from heritage stone houses to modern condominiums on the river, to cottages to standard new subdivisions to nearby estate and farm homes. Prices range from $100,000 for condominiums and nearby cottages, to $150,000 for a modest house in the village to over $800,000 for heritage farms. Lots start at $62,000 and new houses in subdivisions are from $175,000 up.

Employment:

Agriculture and Related	2%
Fishing	0%
Logging	0.2%
Mining and Quarrying	0.3%
Manufacturing	29%
Construction	5%
Transportation and Storage	3%

Communication and Utilities	1%
Wholesale	5%
Retail	12%
Finance/Insurance	3%
Real Estate	2%
Business Service	4%
Government Service	3%
Educational Service	8%
Health and Social Service	9%
Accommodation/Hospitality	7%
Other Services	7%

Average Income of Husband and Wife Family 1996:
$61,423

MEAFORD

1996 Population: 4,681
Web site: http://www.meaford.com
Location:
At the mouth of the Bighead River on Georgian Bay on Highway. 26, three hours north-west of Toronto and a half hour west of Collingwood
Nursing/Retirement Homes:
The Grey County and Owen Sound Housing Authority manages 888 public housing units in Grey County. They are distributed in 32 different housing projects (sites) located in 10 different communities in Grey County. These communities are Chatsworth, Dundalk, Durham, Egremont, Flesherton, Hanover, Markdale, Meaford, Owen Sound and Town of the Blue Mountains (Thornbury). All the units managed are subsidized, rent geared to-income housing units. Approximately 80% of the units (716) house senior citizen, couples or single tenants and 20% of the units (172) are for families.
Other Services:
Co-op Nursery School
Day Care
High School
Junior and Senior Primary Public Schools
Public Library
Seniors' clubs and support services
Ten Churches
Medical Facilities:
Grey Bruce Health Services Hospital; Chiropractic; Dental;

Massage; Home care; Hospice etc.

Recreational Facilities:

Arena
Ball Park
Boat rental
Beaches
Georgian Trail
Marinas
Meaford Museum
Opera House Theatre
Skiing
Swimming Pool
Tennis Courts

Recreation, Sports, Other Groups and Associations:

Apple Harvest Association
Baseball Club
Boat Club
Bowling Club
Camera Club
Concert Series
Coyote Running Club
Community Theatre
Community in Bloom Committee (winner 1999)
Cubs, Scouts
Curling Club
East Grey Hunters and Anglers
Fall Fair
Four H Club
Fishing
Garden Club
Georgian Theatre Festival
Girl Guides
Golf
Hockey Clubs
Horticultural Society
Junior Farmers
Karate Club
Kinsmen
Kiwanis
Lion's Club
Market
Masonic Lodge

Orange Lodge
Royal Canadian Legion
Skateboard Park
Skating Club
Snowmobile Club
Soccer Club
Spanish Club
Steam (engines etc.) club

Other Attractions:

A wide variety of shopping for daily needs as well as antique shops; hand-made jewelry; clothing; art and print galleries; motels, B & Bs; restaurants from gourmet to take-out; craft supplies

Real Estate:

Lots from $100,000 to waterfront estates over $1 million. Numerous chalets and condominiums available nearby from $150,000.

Employment:

Agriculture and Related	5%
Fishing	0%
Logging	0.5%
Mining and Quarrying	0.5%
Manufacturing	13%
Construction	5%
Transportation and Storage	2%
Communication and Utilities	3%
Wholesale	1%
Retail	12%
Finance/Insurance	1%
Real Estate	2%
Business Service	4%
Government Service	5%
Educational Service	7%
Health and Social Service	13%
Accommodation/Hospitality	11%
Other Services	12%

Average Income of Husband and Wife Family 1996:
$50,447

NEUSTADT
1996 Population: 568
Web Site: http://www.ontarioguide.com/gbd/ne_yello.htm

Location:

On Grey Country Road 10 between Hanover and Clifford, two kilometres off Highway 9; an hour and a half north of Guelph and two hours northwest of Toronto

Nursing/Retirement Homes:

One in village; others accessible. The Grey County and Owen Sound Housing Authority manages 888 public housing units in Grey County. They are distributed in 32 different housing projects (sites) located in 10 different communities in Grey County. These communities are Chatsworth, Dundalk, Durham, Egremont, Flesherton, Hanover, Markdale, Meaford, Owen Sound and Town of the Blue Mountains (Thornbury). All the units managed are subsidized, rent geared to-income housing units. Approximately 80% of the units (716) house senior citizens, couples or single tenants and 20% of the units (172) are for families.

Other Services:

Three Churches

Medical Facilities:

Available in Hanover and Clifford

Recreational Facilities:

Arena

Ball Park

Tennis Courts

Recreation, Sports, Other Groups and Associations:

Baseball Club

Curling Club

Hockey Club

Horticultural Society

Other Attractions:

Fall Fair mid-September

Fall Craft Fair early November

Fishing and Hiking along the Saugeen River

Real Estate:

Some small homes in the village available from $80,000. Some nearby farms available for $100,000 up.

Employment:

Agriculture and Related	3%
Fishing	0%
Logging	0%
Mining and Quarrying	0%
Manufacturing	32%
Construction	17%
Transportation and Storage	7%
Communication and Utilities	0%
Wholesale	0%
Retail	22%
Finance/Insurance	3%
Real Estate	0%
Business Service	0%
Government Service	0%
Educational Service	0%
Health and Social Service	7%
Accommodation/Hospitality	6%
Other Services	7%

Average Income of Husband and Wife Family 1996:
$43,664

PAISLEY

1996 Population: 1,106

Web site: http://www.sunsets.com/paisley/

Location:

On Bruce County Road 3, 1.75 hours north of Kitchener and 2.75 hours northwest of Toronto

Nursing/Retirement Homes:

Available in other municipalities through the Bruce County Community Care Access Centre.

Real Estate:

Homes in the village are available from $120,000. Some local farm property is also available from $150,000, but property near Lake Huron is more expensive.

Employment (Arran-Elderslie Municipality):

Agriculture and Related	3%
Fishing	0%
Logging	0%
Mining and Quarrying	0%
Manufacturing	10%
Construction	11%
Transportation and Storage	6%
Communication and Utilities	22%
Wholesale	3%
Retail	18%
Finance/Insurance	0%
Real Estate	0%

Business Service	2%
Government Service	6%
Educational Service	5%
Health and Social Service	4%
Accommodation/Hospitality	5%
Other Services	5%

Average Income of Husband and Wife Family 1996:
$53,521 (Arran-Elderslie Municipality)

ST. JACOBS
1996 Population: 1,515
Web site: http://www.township.woolwich.on.ca/stjacobs.htm
Nursing/Retirement Homes:
A 32 unit senior citizens development is situated on the banks of the Conestogo River along with an 18 acre river front municipal park. Others are widely available through Waterloo Region Community Care Access Centre.
Other Services:
Primary School
Two Churches
Medical Facilities:
The St. Jacobs Community Health Centre offers a broad range of medical services to area residents and access to Hospitals in Kitchener is easy.
Recreational Facilities:
Arena
Ball Park
River Trails
Tennis Courts
Recreation, Sports, Other Groups and Associations:
Baseball Club
Curling Club
Hockey Club
Horticultural Society
Service Clubs
Other Attractions:
A wide range of antique and craft shops, restaurants, markets hotels, motels and B&Bs
Schoolhouse Theatre.

Real Estate:
Houses in the village from $100,000. Some rural properties nearby from $200,000, limited because of Mennonite farming and regional planning restrictions.

Employment (Woolwich Municipality):

Agriculture and Related	12%
Fishing	0%
Logging	0%
Mining and Quarrying	0%
Manufacturing	17%
Construction	8%
Transportation and Storage	3%
Communication and Utilities	2%
Wholesale	7%
Retail	12%
Finance/Insurance	3%
Real Estate	2%
Business Service	4%
Government Service	3%
Educational Service	8%
Health and Social Service	7%
Accommodation/Hospitality	5%
Other Services	9%

Average Family Income of Husband and Wife Family 1996:
$70,938 (Woolwich Municipality)

ST. MARYS
1996 Population: 5,952
Web site: http://www.stonetown.net/town.htm
Location:
At Perth County Roads 123 and 130; 23 kilometres from Stratford and 45 kilometres from London at the junction of the Thames River and Trout Creek; 2.5 hours west of Toronto
Retirement Homes:
Thames valley retirement community — west end of town; 15 acres planned retirement community will accommodate 65 homes when completed; modular homes on leased lots from $136,000. Community center with pool table, fitness centre and library; adjacent to planned commercial area; short distance to hospital and downtown
NURSING/RETIREMENT HOMES:
Wildwood care centre — 24 hour staff, meals, nursing; Kingsway lodge — as above, extended care and retirement home facilities, being enlarged

Other Services:

St. Marys and area home support services: meals on wheels; driving; shopping etc. St. Marys and area association for community living; personal support; planning; advice. The friendship centre: recreational, educational and volunteer opportunities; many programs for persons 50 and over in own building.

Medical Facilities:

St. Marys Memorial Hospital: 24 hour emergency service, 3 year accreditation; modern physiological equipment; colour Doppler ultrasound equipment; featured in *Chatelaine* magazine as "one of the best all-round hospitals in Canada"

Recreational Facilities:

St. Marys Golf and Country club 18 holes; River Valley Golf and Country Club, 9 hole golf course; 8 kilometres west of town, Ryan's Korner mini-putt and fast food

Other Attractions:

Superb historic architecture and picturesque setting in the
   Thames River/Trout Creek valley
St. Marys farmers' market (Saturdays June to November)
Canadian Baseball Hall of Fame and Museum
Wildwood Conservation Area
St. Marys Museum
River walkway
Limestone water tower
Stone and brick cottages and mansions with B&B potential
Scenic drives along the river
Easy access to Stratford and London
Grand Trunk Trail over Sarnia Bridge
A wide variety of shopping for daily needs as well as antique
   shops; hand-made chocolates; art and print galleries;
   hotel, motel, B & Bs; restaurants from gourmet to take-
   out; craft supplies; outfitters, etc.

Recreation, Sports, Other Groups and Association:

See St. Marys and Area Recreation Activities Guide 1999

Real Estate:

New and resale homes are available at prices far below those in larger communities (2.5 story older home 4 bedrooms; $159,000; annual taxes under $2000 for example).

Employment:

Agriculture and Related	5%
Mining and Quarrying	1%
Manufacturing	28%
Construction	4%
Transportation and Storage	3%
Communication and Utilities	0.7%
Wholesale	4%
Retail	15%
Finance/Insurance	2%
Real Estate	2%
Business Service	2%
Government Service	2%
Educational Service	5%
Health and Social Service	13%
Accommodation/Hospitality	6%
Other Services	7%

Average Income of Husband and Wife Family 1996:
$62,323

THORNBURY

1996 Population: 1,763
Web site: http://www.town.thebluemountains.on.ca/
Location:
On Georgian Bay at the Beaver River on Highway 26, half an hour west of Collingwood and 3 hours north west of Toronto
Nursing/Retirement Homes:
Errinrung Nursing Home; the Grey County and Owen Sound Housing Authority manages 888 public housing units in Grey County. They are distributed in 32 different housing projects (sites) located in 10 different communities in Grey County. These communities are Chatsworth, Dundalk, Durham, Egremont, Flesherton, Hanover, Markdale, Meaford, Owen Sound and Town of the Blue Mountains (Thornbury). All the units managed are subsidized, rent geared to-income housing units. Approximately 80% of the units (716) house senior citizen, couples or single tenants and 20% of the units (172) are for families.
Other Services:
Six Churches
Primary Public School
Public Library
Medical Facilities:
Grey Bruce Health Services Hospital in Meaford;

Chiropractic; Dental; Massage; Home care; Hospice etc. in Meaford and Collingwood

Recreational Facilities:

Arena

Five Ball Diamonds

Ten Beaches

Tennis Courts

Recreation, Sports, Other Groups and Associations:

Seventeen associations and clubs, including a soaring club, service clubs, boat clubs etc.

Other Attractions:

Autumn Colours

Boating

Excellent Fishing

Skiing

Superb Hiking and Snowmobile Trails

Real Estate:

Condominiums from $120,000 in town, to larger waterfront estates over $300,000 to several million. Many new chalet and condominium developments in the area.

Employment:

Agriculture and Related 4%

Fishing	0%
Logging	0%
Mining and Quarrying	0%
Manufacturing	7%
Construction	15%
Transportation and Storage	2%
Communication and Utilities	1%
Wholesale	4%
Retail	13%
Finance/Insurance	3%
Real Estate	3%
Business Service	2%
Government Service	5%
Educational Service	3%
Health and Social Service	11%
Accommodation/Hospitality	9%
Other Services	14%

Average Income of Husband and Wife Family 1996:
$44,846

Selected References

Ashenburg, Catherine. 1996. *Going to Town: Architectural Walking Tours in Southern Ontario.* Toronto: Mcfarlane Walter and Ross.

Boyle, Terry. 1991. *Memories of Ontario: The Travellers' Guide to the Towns and Cities of Western Ontario.* Toronto: Cannonbooks.

Chapman, L.J. and D.F. Putnam. 1986. *The Physiography of Southern Ontario.* Toronto: University of Toronto Press (Reprint).

Dahms, F.A. 1977. "How Ontario's Guelph District Developed." *Canadian Geographical Journal,* 94: 48–55.

———. 1988. *The Heart of the Country—From the Great Lakes to the Atlantic Coast: Rediscovering the towns and countryside of Canada.* Toronto: Deneau.

———. 1980. "The Evolving Spatial Organization of Settlements in the Countryside—An Ontario Example." *Tidjschrift voor Econ. en Soc. Geografie,* 71: 295-306.

———. 1980. "Small Town and Village Ontario." Ontario Geography 7/8: 19-32.

———. 1980. "The Evolution of Settlement Systems: A Canadian Example, 1851-1970," *Journal of Urban History* 7: 169-204.

———. 1984. "The process of "urbanization" in the countryside: a study of Bruce and Huron Counties, 1891–1981, *Urban History Review* 12: 1-18.

———. 1984. " 'Demetropolitanization' or the 'urbanization' of the countryside? the changing functions of small rural settlements in Ontario." *Ontario Geography* 24: 35-61.

———. 1986. "Residential and commercial renaissance: another look at small town Ontario." *Small Town* 17: 10-15.

———. 1987. "Regional Urban History: A Statistical and Cartographic Survey of Huron and Southern Bruce Counties." *Urban History Review* 3: 254-268.

———. 1991. "St. Jacobs Ontario: from declining village to thriving tourist community." *Ontario Geography* 36: 1-13.

———. 1991. "Economic Revitalization in St.Jacobs Ontario: Ingredients for Transforming a Dying Village into a Thriving Small Town." *Small Town* 21: 12-18.

———. 1991. "Change and stability within an urban hierarchy: Waterloo County 1864 to 1971." *Urban History Review* 20: 38-47.

———. 1995. "Dying villages, counterurbanization and the urban field – a Canadian perspective." *Journal of Rural Studies* 11: 21-33.

———. 1996. "The greying of south Georgian Bay." *The Canadian Geographer* 40: 148-163.

———. 1998. "Settlement Evolution in the Arena Society in the Urban Field." *Journal of Rural Studies* 14: 299-320.

Dahms, F.A. and J. McComb. 1999. "Counter-urbanization, interaction and function change in an amenity area – a Canadian example." *Journal of Rural Studies* 5: 129-146.

DeVisser, John. 1982. *Southwestern Ontario.* Toronto: Oxford.

Flynn, J. ed. 1999. *The End of an Era: Collingwood Township 1977–1997.* Thornbury: The Town of The Blue Mountains.

Hunter, A.F. 1909. Reprint 1948. *A History of Simcoe County.* Barrie: Simcoe County Historical Society.

Johnston, W.S. and H.J.M Johnston. 1967. *History of Perth County to 1967.* Stratford: Beacon Herald.

Knight, F.S. 1956. *This is Meaford, 1875–1976.* Meaford: Knight Press.

MacDonald, Cheryl, ed. 1992. *Grand Heritage: A History of Dunnville and the Townships of Canborough, Dunn, Moulton, Sherbrooke and South Cayuga.* Dunnville: Dunnville District Heritage Association.

McLeod, N.J. 1969. *The History of the County of Bruce.* Bruce County Historical Society.

Mika, Nick and Helma. 1977. *Encyclopedia of Ontario, Vol II. Places in Ontario.* Belleville: Mika Publishing.

Mitchell C. and F. Dahms eds. 1997. *Challenge and Opportunity: Managing Change in Canadian Towns and Villages.* Waterloo: University of Waterloo Department of Geography Publication No. 48.

Purple Hills Arts and Heritage Society. 1988. *A Green and Pleasant Place: A Glimpse of Creemore and Area.* Creemore.

Regional Municipality of Haldimand-Norfolk. 1998. *H-N Pulse.* Townsend: Regional Administration Building.

Robertson, N. 1906. *The History of the County of Bruce.* Toronto: William Briggs.

Wilson, L.W. and L.R. Pfaff. 1981. *Early St. Marys.* Erin: Boston Mills.

INDEX